AMAZED BY HIS LOVE

Experiencing God's Amazing Love
Through Life's Storms

Terence Andre

Scott,
Be amazed by
His love for you.

Cover design: Mark Hilvert
Editing: Jennifer Lee

Library of Congress Control Number: 2018913458
Kindle Direct Publishing, Seattle, WA

ISBN-13: 978-1728923895

DEDICATION

For Debbie
For thirty-one years together and for the one who lives out the covenant of
"in sickness and in health" every day.
Thank you for the incredible sacrifice you have made in my journey
through leukemia, bone marrow transplant, and brain tumor. You have
loved me with the love of Jesus, without complaint.

CONTENTS

FOREWORD

"Amazing!" It's one of those words like "awesome" and "miraculous." You know, words we tend to throw out there when we don't know what to say. We use them so frequently and casually that they have lost their meaning, and their significance has been diluted. But I contend these are God's words…reserved to refer exclusively to Him and His handiwork. That is why I was so pleased to hear my good friend Terence Andre decided to entitle this book, "Amazed By His Love." What you hold in your hand is not simply a record of one man's journey, it is from cover to cover a testimony of God's amazing, awesome, and miraculous love.

I first met Terence when he and his dear family became part of the church I then pastored in Phoenix, AZ. At the time he was a follower of Jesus. But by his own admission, his faith was rather mechanical at times. Maybe it was his military background that influenced his world-view, but he shared with me that being a Christian was rather "black and white." If you did the right things, you should always expect the right results. He had trusted in Jesus for salvation, but his life had not been completely transformed (another of God's words, cf. Romans 12:1). To put it another way, he had experienced a measure of God's love, but he had really never been amazed by His love. Then life, as it often does, took several unexpected turns that rocked his world and challenged his faith. I watched with a prayerful eye as Terence continued to lean into God through his emotional roller coaster journey and witnessed with great joy the transformation of his life and faith that have allowed those fiery trials to become a platform for God's amazing grace and love.

In this very personal story, I am confident you will be challenged and inspired as you read about an amazing God who can transform fear into faith, despair into hope, and death into life. Be prepared to be amazed by His love.

Mark Fuller
Pastor of Leadership Development
Grove City Church of the Nazarene

ACKNOWLEDGEMENTS

My Lord and Savior, Jesus Christ. He has been with me since I accepted Him as a young boy. And He has walked with me through great affliction and given me all the grace I always needed. I have felt His love like never before in the midst of the story.

To my wife (Debbie), daughter (Jennifer), and sons (Brian and Zachary) for living this story with me and praying me through the really hard times.

Many thanks to the medical team at the University of Colorado Hospital (Anschutz Medical Campus) for your skill and care in treating leukemia.

To my sister, Bonita, who donated her stem cells to make my bone marrow transplant complete and was used by God to heal me of cancer. I will always carry around a part of you, in my blood, for the rest of my life.

My parents (John and Peggy Andre) who taught me at a very young age to trust in God with all my heart.

Debbie's parents (Bruce and Lynda McCaleb) who dropped everything to support us through this journey, even moving in with us to help watch Zachary so Debbie could focus on attending to my needs.

To the hundreds of friends and family members who prayed for me over many years of sickness. Those prayers were felt, and I am here today because of them.

Cathy Oasheim, Oasheim Editing Services, for her review of the first manuscript and helping me connect head to heart in my writing.

To Mark Hilvert who designed the "Amazed" moment on the front cover, representing one night in the hospital where God met me in a special way while listening to the song by the same name.

Many thanks to the company I work for—TiER1 Performance Solutions (www.tier1performance.com). TiER1 is a consulting company with great leaders and colleagues I love to work with. They gave me the time to fight this battle, they fought with me, and they were there at the end to cheer me on past the finish line.

INTRODUCTION

This book is a story of affliction, healing, and transformation. I retired from the Air Force in 2007. Life in the Air Force and in any military service can have its own set of challenges. But for me, I loved serving in the Air Force and had a very rewarding career.

Compared to the story I am about to share, life in the Air Force was easy. Although there were some minor disappointments here and there, the Air Force took care of everything. Movers would come pack us up and deliver our household items at the next assignment. We had great medical care. Wherever the new assignment took us, we would run into friends we had seen at previous locations. The Air Force is a great family to be part of. It helped shape who I am today.

But nothing shaped me more than a serious health challenge several years after I retired—a battle with cancer. This was a fight in unknown territory. Nothing prepared me for this fight, except for my Christian faith. And that faith was going to be tested to extreme limits.

I wrote this book to share my story of affliction and to show that the testing of our faith is not something to run away from. God is particularly watchful over us when we are going through tough times. It is a story that I think touches people in many different ways. It is my testimony of faith in Jesus Christ and how He sustained me, how He rewarded my faith. I am hoping this story will encourage you to consider who Jesus Christ is and what it means to walk with Him in faith.

In the words to come in this book, I hope you will understand more about this phrase, *Amazed by His Love*. The short story of that phrase is this: I have seen that when we really know, when we deeply understand, when we can get our entire mind around how much God loves us, it is transformational. A lot of emotional tension around what angers us, what disappoints us, what frustrates us, starts to melt away and we get an incredible amount of clarity on what really matters. This deep understanding produces an incredible spirit of gratitude and the ability to focus on what we have vs. what we don't have.

Terence Andre, Ph.D.
Chief Scientist, TiER1 Performance Solutions
Colorado Springs, Colorado

CHAPTER ONE

The Beginning of a Journey

I woke up that Sunday morning and was so very weak. You see, I had been in the hospital for seven days. In a few hours, guys from my weekly devotional group were stopping by to do church with me since I couldn't go. I needed their encouragement, but I just wasn't sure if I would have the energy to engage with them.

I texted my friend Todd and said, "Need the encouragement today, but feeling so very weak. I hope I'll be up for it by the time you get here." I left it for him to decide—I couldn't decide if it would be good or bad to have several guys in my room singing songs and sharing some devotions.

On Saturday, a week earlier, I was diagnosed with Acute Myeloid Leukemia. It was a shocking diagnosis. I had never even heard of Acute Myeloid Leukemia. I was told I would be in the hospital for thirty days or so. The first week would involve an intense cocktail of high dose chemotherapy to eradicate the leukemia cells that were in my blood.

That cocktail was meant to go after cancerous white blood cells that were rapidly expanding in my bone marrow. But this treatment couldn't just separate the good cells from the bad cells. It was going to take them all out—good white blood cells, platelets, and red blood cells. These three are the basic ingredients of our blood supply. White blood cells fight off infection, platelets support blood clotting so we don't bleed to death, and red blood cells carry oxygen and give us life.

These cells were all going to be killed off. On that Sunday morning, the cocktail of chemotherapy had taken its toll. My hemoglobin (a measure of my oxygen-carrying red blood cells) was down to critical levels. I was probably going to have a blood transfusion that day to boost my numbers and keep me alive.

This is why I felt so terrible. I had no energy and felt light-headed because I had very few oxygen-carrying red blood cells left. It was a terrible feeling to be left so weak beyond my control. I wanted these guys to come to pray with me, but I also didn't want them to see me this way.

They came anyway and gave me the boost I needed. For about an hour, songs of praise and devotion emanated from my room (the guys called it "man church" in the hospital). I remember seeing some of the nurses passing by my room, and I think they enjoyed the mini church service. It was Sunday and I was in a faith-based hospital.

I ended up spending all of those planned thirty days in the hospital. The first few weeks were grueling. Blood tests twice a day. Blood transfusions about every third day. Bone marrow biopsies—a long needle right into the hipbone to extract out cells from the spongy tissue of large bones. Ouch! But, by the time I reached the fourth week in the hospital, I was actually feeling pretty good—not sick at all. But I couldn't go home.

My immune system was dangerously low, and I needed the doctors, nurses, and medicines to help protect me from infection. There were days I wondered, *how did I get here and what is this all about?*

About a month prior to my diagnosis, I was starting to feel something was wrong. I would normally jog about three miles a few times each week around our neighborhood. One morning, I went for a run and couldn't make it two blocks without gasping for air. I had to walk the rest of the way. I wondered if I had a bad cold or something that was clogging me up. I felt tired all the time.

The week before my diagnosis, my wife (Debbie) and I went on a weekend getaway to the historic Hotel Boulderado in Boulder, Colorado, a gift from the company I worked for—TiER1 Performance Solutions (more on TiER1 in Chapter 9). The company founders (Greg Harmeyer, Kevin Moore, and Norm Desmarais) sent Debbie and I a gift certificate for two nights at the Boulderado for Christmas 2009. The hotel opened in 1909 in downtown Boulder. On one of his trips to Colorado, Kevin Moore tells me that he drove up to Boulder, checked out the hotel, and bought the gift certificate on behalf of TiER1. We had won several large research grants in 2009, and Greg, Kevin, and Norm wanted to send me a meaningful message that they valued the achievement, and me. It was an amazing gift, especially for Debbie. She had never seen anything like this in my working career. The Air Force doesn't send you gift cards for high achievement—they sometimes give you a medal for your uniform or hand you a printed certificate recognizing outstanding achievement, but no money is involved.

So, in February 2010, Debbie and I drove up to Boulder to stay at this beautiful hotel. We checked in at the lobby desk and noticed an old elevator nearby as we prepared to head upstairs to our room; it had a sign on it that said, "Please ask a staff member for assistance." It turns out this was the original Otis elevator installed in 1908, and it was still working. We decided we didn't want to wait for a staff member, so we took the beautiful stairs up four floors to our room. On the way up, I noticed I was having a difficult time going up the stairs. It was the same feeling I had on my runs in recent weeks. At the top of the first flight of stairs, I asked Debbie if we could take a break—I was out of breath. At the top of each floor, I had to take a break and catch my breath. I couldn't figure out why I was struggling. We wrote it off as maybe the beginning signs of a cold and enjoyed the rest of our time at this beautiful hotel.

We got back from Boulder, and I decided that I should

probably get checked out by a doctor. The following Tuesday I made an appointment with my doctor at the Air Force Academy hospital. The doctor looked me over and asked all kinds of questions. He wasn't sure what was wrong. He suggested it might be some type of virus. He decided to take a blood test to get a complete blood count (CBC).

I went to the lab to have them draw some blood and then sat down to wait. About an hour later I was called back in by my doctor. He looked pretty serious. He said that my CBC was very unusual. My white blood count was off the charts. It was 45,000 (normal is 4,000 to 8,000). My platelets were down to 90,000 (normal is 150,000 to 450,000). And my hemoglobin was down to 10.5 (normal is 13.0 to 16.0).

This explained why I was feeling so weak and tired. I had a significantly reduced level of oxygen-carrying red blood cells. The doctor said he had only seen a count like this one other time and it was someone who had an extreme viral infection. Even though that was hard to hear, at least it was a possible answer and antibiotics should take care of that.

He recommended that I see a hematologist right away. He knew a good hematologist in town and initiated the paperwork for me to be seen later that week. The doctor worked at a cancer center in town, and for some reason I didn't give that any thought. I wasn't even thinking in the realm of cancer. I was hooked on the idea of this being a viral infection.

On Friday of that week, I went to see this hematologist. At the appointment, they collected blood in order to do a CBC, as expected. The doctor called me in once the results were back from the lab. He asked me lots of questions and then turned his attention to the CBC results. They were still way out of whack. White blood cells were growing, while platelets and hemoglobin were decreasing.

Like the Air Force doctor, he said this could be any number of things. And then he said, "and some of those possibilities include scary things like blood cancers." That was the first time anyone had mentioned the possibility of cancer. *I'm just feeling a little off, a little tired*, I thought. *How could this be cancer in the blood?*

The doctor said, "The only way to tell for sure is to do a bone marrow biopsy." I had heard of biopsies before, but wondered what a bone marrow biopsy was all about. It didn't sound good. *How do you get a sample of the bone marrow?* I thought. He explained the procedure to me and sure enough, it didn't sound good. A long needle has to be inserted into the hipbone and some fluid and some of the spongy part of the bone is extracted. The doctor told me he could do this right after lunch that day. I quickly called Debbie and asked if she could come down for that biopsy—I didn't want to go through that alone.

Debbie and I met for lunch and quickly headed back to the cancer center for this biopsy. I was instructed to lie down and was given a pillow. As it was explained to me, the doctor would numb a spot on my back side just above my hipbone. I would feel some of that, but it would mostly be like a bee sting. But once they got to the spongy part of the bone, there was really no way to numb that. I would feel every bit of it could only "hang on for the ride."

I guess that was what the pillow was for—to cry like a baby right into that comforting pillow. As they began the procedure, I heard the doctor ask my wife if she was okay. The shock of the type of instrument they were going to use on me was quite overwhelming for her (I never saw it). Debbie got a little light headed and was about to pass out. I heard the nurse take her out of the room to get some fresh air and some water. I was on my own now.

It was quite a ride of pain once the doctor reached the bone marrow with the needle and extracted out the required amount of fluid and material. I did hang on to that pillow for dear life. What seemed like a very long procedure was probably done in about fifteen minutes. A patch was put over the site and we were told that the sample would be rushed to a lab in California. We were also told that the results should be back in 24 hours.

CHAPTER TWO

You Have Leukemia

Our family was having a relaxing Saturday evening. We were watching the 2010 Winter Olympics that February when the phone rang. I went upstairs to get it. On the other end of the line was a doctor from the clinic I was at the day before where I had the bone marrow biopsy.

He said, "Mr. Andre, we don't typically make these calls on the weekend unless we see something serious in your biopsy results. We just got your results back and you have Acute Myeloid Leukemia." In that moment, the world seemed to stop. I think I was trying to get my head around what the doctor just said. I had heard the word "leukemia" before and typically associated it with children. In fact, an image of a child in the hospital, bald, going through treatment, came to mind. But I don't think I ever heard of it in the context of adults. I knew in my mind that it could be a catastrophic disease. I think the doctor paused for a moment as he could tell I was stunned. He then continued with more information.

He walked me through the seriousness of Acute Myeloid Leukemia and told me that I would need to come into the hospital Monday morning to be treated for this disease. He explained that I should take the rest of the weekend to prepare for this long stay in the hospital. That involved getting things packed, letting my company know I would be gone for several weeks, and bringing our medical information to the hospital. He mentioned that most people have to spend at least four weeks in the hospital, sometimes longer. I was writing down all these facts almost as if I were going to pass this along to someone else, but somehow trying to process that this was about me!

While I was on the call, Debbie came upstairs to see what the call was about. I whispered to her that a doctor was talking to me and that he says that I have leukemia. I could just see her spirit deflate and she basically collapsed into a chair in our living room.

As soon as the doctor was done talking to me, I sat down with her and explained everything I heard. She started researching Acute Myeloid Leukemia on her computer and I could tell she was coming across overwhelming information. She looked at me and said, "This is not good." The more we researched online, the deeper our hearts sank. This was a very serious diagnosis and the outcomes did not look good. After a few minutes of researching Acute Myeloid Leukemia, we both looked at each other and realized we needed to go downstairs and tell our children.

We gathered ourselves together as best we could, went downstairs, and Debbie called the kids together and said, "Daddy has a very serious disease called Acute Myeloid Leukemia. Most people just call it leukemia. It is cancer."

Hearing her say that word was devastating. I can't remember what our kids said, but I know they were stunned. How do you process something like this? They were probably thinking, "Does this mean Daddy is going to die?" No one said that, but I could tell that was the mood in our home at that moment. I tried to look at my children without a lot of worry on my face so they would somehow see my faith in God and be comforted by His presence at that moment. Deep down I knew this was serious. You don't get any training on handling situations like this. All I knew to do was to try my best to hold it together. If I lost it, it would make the night even tougher for them. I paused in my heart and offered a silent prayer, "Lord help me to remain calm—give me your peace."

I remember making lots of phone calls that night. We called our parents; Debbie's parents in Colorado Springs and my parents in Sacramento. We called some close friends. One of our friends quickly told us we needed to set up a Caring Bridge website where we could update our network without having to write and reply to lots of emails. We had never heard of Caring Bridge before, but Debbie started looking into it.

Somehow, we got the kids to bed that night and were able to get some sleep, although both Debbie and I were restless all night. A lot was racing through our minds.

On Sunday morning, we went to church with Debbie's parents so we could all be together. The pastor had us come up front and people gathered around us to pray. Our hearts were encouraged by this prayer, but the journey ahead was still overwhelming, unknown, and very scary. This was new territory for our family. All of us lived relatively healthy lives with very little hospital stays. Thirty days in the hospital, plus everything beyond that was such unknown territory.

After church, we came home and had lunch. I remember getting on a conference call with the founders of our company (Greg, Kevin, and Norm) and told them what was going on and that I would be going into the hospital the next morning for what was likely a thirty-day stay. The founders of the company quickly took on the responsibility of passing my work assignments onto other people and encouraged me to focus on getting better. They were committed to taking the stress of work off of me and told me not to worry about anything at work. The conversation provided much needed reassurance and encouragement.

The rest of Sunday is somewhat fuzzy in our memory. We grabbed everything we could think of for staying in the hospital for thirty days. We made a lot of phone calls and tried our best to prepare for something so unknown. Debbie's parents came that Sunday night to stay with us and essentially move in as we recognized how much help we would need at home while Debbie became my primary caregiver in the hospital over the next several weeks. The help was especially important because our youngest, Zachary, was three years old at the time.

Our oldest, Jennifer (20), was in her last semester at a local college. Brian, seventeen at the time, was finishing high school through a homeschooling program, attending a local community college for both high school and college credits, and preparing to attend the United States Air Force Academy. Just a month earlier, Brian received an appointment to the Air Force Academy; our entire family was elated and proud. The contrast between that fabulous news and what we were facing now was a dramatic emotional shift.

Debbie and I got to the hospital the next morning for me to be admitted. I didn't know it at the time, but this hospital in Colorado Springs—Penrose Hospital—would become my home for the next thirty days.

It seemed like the longest day in our lives. It was nearly evening before I was settled into a room because of all the blood tests, x-rays, and a surgical procedure to put a port in for administering fluids, medicine, and chemo. Debbie left late that night after she felt assured that I was in good hands for my first evening in the hospital.

I was now alone in a hospital room with all kinds of things hooked up to my body to begin the chemo treatment the next day. I'm not sure I really understand what was in front of me. I looked at the beautiful view of Pikes Peak out my window and prayed that God would help me take one day at a time without being consumed with all that could go wrong. While I began my journey of chemo treatments, Debbie would begin her journey of trying to manage things at home and spend time with me each day for the next thirty days.

CHAPTER THREE

Thirty Days

For the next thirty days, I learned a lot about hospitals and nursing. When you are in a hospital twenty-four hours a day for thirty days, you start to learn a great deal about the shift schedules, what's good and what's bad on the food menu, the personalities of the nurses, and the scheduling of tests and lab work. Debbie and I both enjoyed good conversations with doctors and nurses, learning about their background and families, hearing their stories of how they got into the medical field, and receiving insight on how to handle the medical journey we were just beginning. Debbie was there every day. She tried to be there by 8:00 a.m. every morning and stayed until about 6:00 p.m. We both felt it was important for her to be home at night to put Zachary to bed. In the evening, Debbie, along with Jennifer, Brian, and Debbie's parents (Bruce and Lynda), would plan out the next day's schedule. She would tell them what went on at the hospital that day so they could stay up with my care. Our children would come a couple times each week to see me. I always enjoyed seeing them come into the room—a highlight to break up the long days in the hospital.

A new experience I found in this hospital is that I could

actually order from a menu for breakfast, lunch, and dinner. The last time I was in a hospital as a patient was when I was in high school, to remove my appendix. From that experience, and the experiences with Debbie in the hospital for the births of our children, I don't remember having the option to order what you wanted. A patient basically got what they were serving that day. So, this was new and somewhat exciting. Well, at least for a few weeks. After a couple of weeks in the hospital, this new experience started to wear off. I got tired of the same things repeating on the menu. When my immune system reached bottom from all the chemo treatments, I had to go on a limited diet with no fresh fruits. All of my food had to be cooked to a specific temperature and carefully delivered to my room, covered in plastic wrap. And then, all of a sudden, I started to develop an intense craving for Chili's™ chips and salsa. I love Chili's™ chips and salsa—they have found, in my opinion, the optimal combination of salty chips and tangy salsa. I guess it is when you can't have something (i.e., fresh salsa) that you start to crave that food item. I casually mentioned the craving to one of my nurses one morning, and on my lunch plate that day was a sealed bag of chips and heated salsa that the cafeteria prepared just for me. I will always remember that act of service as a personal message to me from the nursing staff that I was valued as a patient.

My thirty days in the hospital was probably toughest on Zachary. He was three at the time and really didn't understand what was going on. I could tell Debbie was in a tough spot—she needed to come spend time with me in the hospital each day, yet she also needed to care for Zachary. This tension was an incredible tug on Debbie's heart. One story we all remember well gives a picture of what was going on in Zachary's heart at the time.

About three weeks into my stay, Debbie was driving home from the hospital and got a call on her cell phone from Brian. But it wasn't Brian on the other end of the call. It was Zachary, our three-year old! He didn't even know how to use a cell phone (or so we thought!). After dinner, he went downstairs into Brian's room, pushed a button on his cell phone (it must have been the button to dial the last number), and called Debbie's number. He said "Mommy, I want to see you, when will you be home?" Stunned, Debbie told him she would be home in a few minutes. He then said, "Mommy, I will leave the phone on and read Berenstain Bears books to you until you get home." He so sweetly wanted to "keep Mommy company" as he eagerly waited for her to return. Debbie felt his loneliness, and she tried to get him to hang up and find Grandma or Grandpa or Sissy or Brother, but Zachary began crying, not wanting to end the call (and not sure how). Debbie had to call her father at our house and tell him that Zachary was downstairs crying because he didn't know how to hang up the phone. It was both adorably funny and a poignant reminder that even 3-year old Zachary was deeply impacted by this journey.

As I was nearing the thirty-day point, I had to have another bone marrow biopsy. This biopsy was to check if the chemo treatments had worked to eliminate the leukemia cells and confirm I was in remission. A couple days after that, my leukemia doctor (Dr. Murphy) came in and gave us good news: the treatments had eliminated leukemia in my blood and I could go home soon! The news of being released soon brought so much excitement and anticipation of finally walking out of a hospital and sleeping in my own bed.

I was released from the hospital in March 2010, exactly thirty days after starting treatment. It seemed like it took the better part of a day to get released. The charge nurse had to spend a significant amount of time with us going over medications, what I could/couldn't eat, and how to take care of my port for future chemo treatments. Dr. Murphy went over the schedule for future consolidation treatments. As it was explained to me, I just completed what was called induction treatment. The purpose of induction treatment is to eliminate as many leukemia cells as possible. Consolidation treatment is used to destroy any remaining leukemia cells and help prevent a relapse. Dr. Murphy explained that I would likely have four consolidation treatments where I would come back to the hospital each time and receive chemo treatments over a seven-day period. There would be about a month between each treatment. Even though I would face four of these treatments, seven days sounded so much better than thirty days. I felt like I could easily handle that after what I had been through.

I remember the moment I walked into our house after being gone for thirty days. The smell of the house and the familiarity was so refreshing—I didn't realize how much I missed it until that moment. For the first few minutes, I felt a wave of joy sweep over me and I blinked back a few tears that started to come. *I was home and I was going to be ok.*

I could tell I was a lot weaker after spending a month in a hospital room with no physical activity. But I quickly fell into my normal routine, working out of my home office and enjoying time with my family. A few things were different though. I was at risk for infection because of my weakened immune system, so I had to be careful what I ate, especially away from home. Salad bars and food that was not fully cooked were off limits. Fresh fruits and vegetables had to be carefully washed before I could eat them. And I needed to guard against being around anyone who was sick. I stayed home often or wore a mask and avoided shaking hands in public.

The next four weeks went way too fast. It was now time for me to go back to the hospital for my first consolidation treatment. It was strange walking back into that same hospital, not feeling sick. In one way, it felt like I was checking into a hotel for a short stay. I quickly established a routine for each time I was in the hospital for these consolidation treatments: ordering the same food, walking the halls for physical activity, and going to bed and getting up at similar times. I even established a regular work routine—taking phone calls and working on research proposals and supporting some projects. A few times, the nurses unhooked me from my IV pole so I could go down into the courtyard and enjoy being outside in the sun for a few hours. I was thinking, *why am I here—I could be doing this at home?* The reason I had to be in the hospital, as my doctor explained, is that the chemo treatments had to be carefully controlled and I needed to be watched closely for any adverse reaction during each 7-day treatment.

We had some flexibility in scheduling each of the four consolidation treatments, approximately a month apart. Because of that, I didn't miss any significant events happening in our family. In May, I was able to attend Jennifer's college graduation, and later that evening, I attended Brian's graduation from high school. In June, I was even able to accompany the whole family to Brian's in-processing day at the Air Force Academy (the beginning of a four-year journey for him). Attending those events made it feel like I was not facing a catastrophic illness—that helped bring some sense of normalcy around was I was facing. And I know it helped soften any disappointment Jennifer and Brian might have felt over having a sick Dad.

One of the significant risks my doctor told me about was the possibility of infection after each treatment. The chemo knocked down my blood counts and each time, my immune system was compromised. I received many blood transfusions during this time to boost my red blood cell count and platelet count. But there was nothing the doctors could give me to increase my white cell count—the cells responsible for fighting infection. That is one of the reasons I had to stay in the hospital for so long, especially during the thirty-day induction treatment. Now that I was doing these treatments with only seven days in the hospital, I had to be very careful during the month I was out of the hospital between treatments. I felt really good going into my fourth treatment in August 2010. I had not developed an infection, and this was going to be the last one. I completed the final seven-day treatment in the hospital and went home. About a week after completing my last treatment, I started to have a headache and I felt hot. Debbie checked my temperature several times a day and monitored me closely. We were instructed to call the hospital if my temperature went above 100.5 degrees. I called Debbie into the bedroom and had her check my temperature. It was 100 degrees. We stopped and prayed right then that this would not be a sign of infection. I could tell there was concern on her face. I was concerned also. We let another hour go by and she checked it again. My temperature had risen to 100.5. It was time to call the hospital. They instructed us to come in right away. So, we packed a bag for me and headed to the hospital, not knowing what was ahead since this was the first time this happened.

After waiting in the ER for hours, I was admitted back to the blood cancer floor I had been on for induction treatment and four consolidation treatments. I didn't want to be back. I made it through all the treatments and wanted to tell a great story of God's faithfulness that I never developed a fever. But God's story is often different than ours. I spent another week in the hospital as I received a ton of IV antibiotics to fight an infection. I must have been hooked up to five or six IV bags as the medical team of doctors and specialists tried to diagnose the infection, deliver antibiotics, and provide other medications to help me get to the other side of the infection. With the four consolidation treatments, and the trip back to the hospital because of the infection, I spent another thirty-five days in the hospital during 2010—sixty-five days total to battle through the fight with leukemia.

CHAPTER FOUR

Time for a Donor

I continued to have blood checks about once a month after consolidation treatment to make sure everything was ok. In February 2011, I had a regular blood check and the numbers didn't look right. This was exactly a year after my original diagnosis. I felt fine, certainly a lot better than before the original diagnosis a year earlier. But my doctor didn't like the numbers. He performed another bone marrow biopsy. The next day we received a call from him that it showed very early evidence that leukemia was coming back. I was stunned, and it rocked our family again. We were just starting to build the confidence, with each new day where I felt good, that leukemia was behind us. It was especially difficult to hear this news knowing that my doctor had told us the first week in the hospital that I had a type of leukemia that was very treatable. This was certainly a time to shake our faith again. We could feel fear rising in our hearts again. But we went right to the methods we had used before—we went to prayer and asked God to be with us through this next part of the journey. This verse in Psalm 56:3 reminded us of where to place our fears: "When I am afraid, I put my trust in you." There were a lot of questions in our mind about what this meant, but from our experience over the past year, we knew we couldn't get too far out in front of our thoughts. We had learned to trust God and that He would be with us in every step.

Deep in our hearts we somehow knew that it is not good news to have a relapse of leukemia. My only option now was to consider a bone marrow transplant. My doctor recommended that we meet with a bone marrow transplant specialist at the University of Colorado Hospital, Anschutz Campus in Denver, Colorado. In fact, my doctor called ahead to this specialist and got us an appointment the next day. Debbie and I drove up to that appointment having no idea of what was ahead. I remember driving into the parking lot at the hospital and seeing the sign, "Anschutz Cancer Pavilion." That word, *cancer*, hit me hard. *What was I doing here? I don't have cancer, I just have leukemia.* I'm not sure why I thought of them differently, but the word, cancer, was just not used a lot around me during my battle with leukemia. Leukemia is a blood cancer, but I had not wrapped my mind around what that fully meant. One other memory I have of that first drive onto the Anschutz campus is how big it was. It did not have the feel of Penrose Hospital—a very quiet, local hospital where you could easily find parking. Anschutz was massive with buildings all around us and hundreds of cars trying to find a parking spot. I could feel the seriousness of this place as we walked toward the doors.

Debbie and I were brought to a room soon after we checked in. A few minutes later, three doctors walked in. One was Dr. Gutman—a highly regarded physician specializing in bone marrow transplant. The other two were residents in training. The Anschutz campus is a teaching hospital, and we would soon learn that there were a lot of resident physicians at this hospital. I remember the look on Dr. Gutman's face as he came in—he was very focused, business-like as he began to tell us what bone marrow transplant was all about. He began by saying, "We all recognize you are here for a very serious condition." The meeting was technical with details of what the process would involve, how long I would stay in the hospital, and what the recovery would look like. One thing we quickly learned is that this would be a stem cell transplant—an infusion of a donor's cells into my blood that would replace my bone marrow. I had in my mind that "bone marrow transplant" involved surgery. I think I got that image from an old movie where I remembered something about how bone marrow transplant was done—in an operating room where bone marrow was surgically removed from the donor and put into the recipient. Stem cell transplant, as we learned, was not so invasive. Stem cells are collected from the blood of the donor, instead of from the actual bone marrow. The recipient receives those new stem cells through an IV into a vein, and waits for those stem cells to graft to the bone marrow and produce new red blood cells, platelets, and white blood cells.

For this transplant process, I would likely be in the hospital for about a month. Dr. Gutman described transplant day as Day 0. Seven days before that (Day -7) I would come into the hospital and start a regimen of high dose chemotherapy. On Day 0, the day of transplant, I would receive a dose of whole body radiation. The purpose of those seven days was to knock the leukemia cells in my bone marrow down to nearly zero in order to reduce the chances that my body would fight off the new stem cells. The whole body radiation was intended to be the last intense shock to my bone marrow as an insurance policy that all leukemia cells were destroyed and that the chances of rejection were very small. At that time, I had no idea what whole body radiation meant, but it sounded intimidating. After that seven-day process, I would stay in the hospital for likely another three weeks until the stem cells attached to my bone marrow and started making new red blood cells, white blood cells, and platelets, all coded with the donor's DNA. The time frame for recovery in the hospital after transplant was approximate because it would all depend on when my immune system recovered. I needed a healthy count of white blood cells before I could be released from the hospital.

The last thing Dr. Gutman told us is the we would have to stay near the hospital for three months after transplant. As he explained, there were all kinds of serious complications that could happen after transplant. He referred to transplant rejection as "Graft-versus-Host-Disease" or GVHD. GVHD is a complication that can happen when the donor's new stem cells (the graft) reject or see my body (the host) as foreign. GVHD can vary from minor complications (skin rash, dry mouth, swelling, nausea, diarrhea) to serious complications (liver damage, shortness of breath, joint problems, and even death). Because of these complications, I had to live within fifteen minutes of the hospital so that any complications could be quickly addressed. These logistics of moving to Denver wasn't even on our radar coming into this meeting.

After this technical explanation, Dr. Gutman asked if we had any questions. I was so overwhelmed with the details, I couldn't think of where to start. After a few seconds of silence, Debbie spoke up and asked, "What are the chances of survival for transplant?" Just like that—she asked a very direct and important question. Dr. Gutman paused for a moment and looked directly at us and said, "On average we see about a 50 percent survival rate from transplant." We were both shocked. Somehow we had just figured transplant would be a 100 percent cure, and all would be fine. The new realization that there was a high chance I may not make it—that this relapse could mean death—washed over both of us, overwhelming our hearts with heaviness.

Was I going to make it? What would we tell the kids? How would we live in Denver, an hour away from our home? Who would take care of Zachary? He was four at the time. How would Jennifer and Brian handle life back in Colorado Springs without us? Jennifer, now 21, was living at home and working as a teacher at a middle school. Brian, now 19, was just finishing his first year at the Air Force Academy. What would happen if I didn't make it? How would Debbie do life without me, and how would Zachary grow up without a Dad? We knew God was in control, but everything felt so impossible and out of control.

The next few weeks seemed to rush by. Much of that time

was working with my medical team at Anschutz to find a donor. A standard part of bone marrow transplant is to test your siblings before going out to the national network of donors to see if there is a match. I only have one sibling, Bonita, who lives in Sacramento. They sent her a blood kit, and it eventually made it back to the University of Colorado Hospital for analysis, where the transplant would occur. I still remember Dr. Gutman sending me an email that Bonita was a perfect match—he was very encouraged by this news, and so were we. I was told by my medical team that there is only a 25 percent chance that any one sibling will be a match, and she was a perfect match—the best outcome anyone could hope for. Finding a match is the most critical part of surviving bone marrow transplant. And if the DNA of that match comes from a family member, versus a donor match in the general population, it reduces the chances of serious GVHD complications, and increases the chances of survival.

God was at work, both in my life and in the life of my sister to bring this together. Once we confirmed that my sister was a match, the process accelerated. I had to go back to Penrose Hospital for another round of chemo to get me back into remission before I could begin the transplant process. Most of the recovery was at home for this round of chemo, but I did develop another infection and had to spend ten more days at Penrose Hospital. After the infection was resolved, the Anschutz medical team scheduled the transplant process to begin on April 4, 2011. We flew my sister out to Denver to prepare for her part being my donor. My sister was scared of the process, but she knew she was doing an incredible thing by donating her stem cells to save my life. She had to come to the Anschutz hospital campus around Day -5 to receive daily shots that would help her stem cells move from her bone marrow into the blood. These shots also helped to increase the number of stem cells needed for transplant. I knew that would be tough on Bonita—she hates needles! She would tell me later on that the only way she got through it was the thought of saving my life.

Debbie, Zachary, and I moved into an apartment on the Anschutz campus about two days before I was admitted. The weeks leading up to that move were intense. Debbie took on the pressure of thinking through all that we would need to have with us for a three-month stay in a small apartment. Debbie's parents (Bruce and Lynda) also moved to Denver so Zachary could be cared for while Debbie spent time with me in the hospital. Bruce and Lynda lived with us in the apartment during the week, and Jennifer would come up to the apartment on the weekends to help with Zachary.

We were encouraged by the outpouring of support from our friends and neighbors back in Colorado Springs, and across the country, for the move up to Denver. We sent out a list of items needed for the apartment on our Caring Bridge site. Within a matter of days of that request going out, we started to see items arrive at our house that would help make our stay in Denver more comfortable. A friend of mine who was the CEO of a home building company in Colorado Springs let us use some furniture out of a model home. Our church provided an extra freezer to store food that was given by friends and church members. Our neighbors took turns cleaning our house and making sure everything around the house was secure.

Debbie and I checked into the hospital on April 4, 2011. We were directed to the eleventh floor of Anschutz—the bone marrow transplant unit. I remember walking into that room and wondering if I would ever walk out again. We knew this was a very serious situation with a lot of risks where things could go wrong. That evening, I started another round of chemo to begin the 7-day preparation process. On April 11, 2011 (Day 0), I went through full body radiation so that my system would not reject the stem cells I was preparing to receive from my sister later that day. The transplant staff prepared my sister in another part of the hospital, so that her stem cells could be collected and given to me much like a blood transfusion.

The process for Bonita involved inserting an IV line to

remove the part of the white blood cells that contain stem cells, separate them using a machine, and then put those stem cells in a transfusion bag. Even though this did not involve surgery, Bonita had to be strong for all the needles and poking. She was doing a very brave thing and giving me an incredible gift. I didn't know it at the time, but she was struggling that day, several floors below where I was located. I wondered what was taking so long because it was getting late into the evening and there was no sign of my nursing team or the stem cells. As it turns out, the medical staff was having a hard time getting the IV into her arm. In addition to hating needles, Bonita once told me that her veins seemed to be tougher for nurses to work with. She was ready to give up from the exhausting struggle of trying to find a vein that worked. Because of the difficulty and the drain on Bonita emotionally, the nurses called in Dr. Gutman. Dr. Gutman came in and told Bonita they would have to find another place to insert the IV, and that place would be in her neck. Dr. Gutman could see her hesitation and said, "Bonita, if you don't do this, your brother is not going to make it. Let us proceed so we can save his life." Bonita leaned in and responded, "Ok, let's do this." Bonita mustered the courage and stepped into an incredibly intense situation that would be a defining moment for her.

Around 9:30 that night I received my sister's stem cells. The nurses brought in the small bag of stem cells from Bonita and let me look at it before they started the transfusion. Even my doctor was there in case something serious went wrong. Immediate rejection can be the most serious result to watch for. But that did not happen.

Over the next 18 days, the stem cells from my sister would engraft and start building new red and white blood cells and platelets. I was discharged from the hospital after 25 days. I didn't have much of an immune system, so I joined Debbie, her parents, and Zachary in the apartment for another two months until it was safe to go home. Jennifer and Brian visited as much as they could. They had busy schedules in Colorado Springs and could only make it up to Denver during short breaks or on weekends. Debbie went home one night each week to check on the house.

The number of pills I was given for those two months was overwhelming. There were probably 30 pills I had to take each day, mostly because of possible rejection of the transplant and to handle infections. I experienced some minor effects of GVHD. Mostly dry mouth, some nausea, and swelling. One concept I learned from my doctor about GVHD while in the hospital was that a low level of GVHD can actually be beneficial. This is because the immune system that attacks the host (my bone marrow) causing GVHD is also known to attack cancer cells. Research has found that patients with a minor case of GVHD generally have a lower risk of having a relapse of their cancer. I tried to view my minor case of GVHD as evidence that the transplant was at work fighting any remaining leukemia cells, even though it did cause some discomfort.

After two months in the apartment, we were given the option to move back home at the beginning of July 2011. Dr. Gutman said we could go home as long as I came back weekly for blood checks, avoided public places, and made sure I was not around anyone sick. I still had a compromised immune system, but the most dangerous time was behind us. Arriving home was so wonderful, but also scary. I was no longer minutes away from the bone marrow transplant unit. It would take us an hour to get there if something happened. It felt like a step of faith to not be so dependent on the hospital being a few minutes away. But our confidence and strength grew as life slowly got back to normal. Again, we leaned into trusting God for every day and tried not to let our thoughts get out of control.

Slowly I began to feel better and started to taper off many of the medicines I was prescribed after transplant. By September 2011, I was starting to feel almost normal. But it was almost a full year before I was off all the medicines from transplant and felt 100 percent normal. There were low points of feeling weak, low appetite, and even fear of what could happen if the transplant didn't take. But, looking back, I remember thinking that I expected the journey to be much worse considering what we were first told. The worst case scenarios just never happened.

Looking back at 2010 and 2011, I counted over 130 nights in the hospital and 40 blood transfusions. Plus, many rounds of chemo and then total body radiation. It was a miracle to be alive. God still wasn't done with me and there was more to learn from this experience. Bone marrow transplant transformed me spiritually in a way I never imagined. I think the many days I spent in the hospital gave lots of quiet time to reflect on my life, to consider what God was whispering to me, and for our family to grow together during a very difficult time.

CHAPTER FIVE

Can You Really Be Transformed

After my experience with bone marrow transplant, I began to ask as a believer in Jesus Christ, "Can a person really be transformed spiritually?" Isn't that a silly question? Of course, the answer to the question is a resounding "Yes." But if we are really honest, it is easy to have doubts around real spiritual transformation. We can even think, *This part of my life can be transformed, but I am not so sure about that part.* Or, *I've tried a dozen times to work this part out of my life, but it just never sticks.*

We believe in what Jesus did on the cross, and we also believe He is coming back again. We know that He has saved us from our sins and He has enormous grace for us as we continue to stumble. But we just can't get fully to the point of real transformation in some parts of our life. So even though the obvious answer to "can you really be transformed?" is yes, reality is that we have some doubt. Not always and not everyone, but this happens more than we would like to think as believers.

A few months after transplant, I was reading in Luke 22. I came to these words:

> "And he took bread, gave thanks and

broke it, and gave it to them, saying,
'This is my body given for you; do this
in remembrance of me.' In the same
way, after the supper he took the cup,
saying, 'This cup is the new covenant in
my blood, which is poured out for
you.'" (Luke 22:19-20)

For some reason, God stopped me on the words "new covenant," especially the word *new*. *What is new, I thought, and what am I to get out of that verse?* Those words made me think of my own experience dealing with blood cancer.

When leukemia came back, my only hope was a bone marrow transplant. My blood was going to kill me. It was death to me. Through the grace of God, my only sibling, my sister, was found to be a perfect match for me. The goal of bone marrow transplant is to be 100% donor converted in your bone marrow. It is typically not a good outcome to have both diseased DNA and donor stem cell DNA mixed in the bone marrow. Every year when I have my labs done, the clinical staff does a complete blood panel. One of the tests is to see if there is any evidence of my diseased blood DNA. With a female donor, there is an easy way to check. We all have 23 pairs of chromosomes with the gender chromosome listed as an XY (male) or XX (female). In my case, the result comes back as 46 XX. These numbers and letters mean there are 23 pairs of chromosomes with the gender chromosome now an XX (female). But here is the line of the lab result that always impacts me: "no evidence of pre-bone marrow transplant host disease." Right before I accepted my sister's stem cells, the hospital took a sample of my bone marrow with diseased leukemia in it. Now, when they do this test each year, they compare that sample from April 2011 to the current sample. This test has the ability to see if there is any of the diseased marrow left in my body and the conclusion is absolutely not! *There is no evidence of the former diseased blood.*

When we accept Christ into our lives and He forgives us of our sins, He is essentially giving us a spiritual bone marrow transplant. We are taking on His identity by accepting Him as Lord of our lives. The Apostle Paul says it this way:

"God made him who had no sin to be
sin for us, so that in him we might
become the righteousness of God." (2
Corinthians 5:21)

How can that be, you ask? It is just like the lab test I receive each year that says, "no evidence of your previous disease." The evidence of that test essentially shows that I have my sister's blood DNA composition. When we accept Christ, God now looks upon us and sees the spiritual DNA composition of Jesus. He doesn't see our previous diseased life! Our old life has been made pure by Jesus—Jesus' "spiritual bone marrow transplant." We are new just as Paul says it in 2 Corinthians:

"Therefore, if anyone is in Christ, the
new creation has come. The old has
gone, the new is here." (2 Corinthians
5:17)

While reflecting on this idea of being a "new creation," I felt a deep impression that God was saying to me, "Don't you think if I can design your body in such a way and give medical science the ability to do this miraculous transformation of the physical blood that I can figure out a way to do the same transformation in the spiritual realm?" What an incredible thought!

I certainly have no doubt about the physical transformation that happened to me in April 2011. Given that we serve the creator of the universe and all that happened through Jesus, why do we have any doubt that real spiritual transformation can occur? We shouldn't have any doubt. We just need to receive it, believe that it is done, and live a life that is holy and pleasing to God (see Romans 12:1). Real transformation is REALLY possible.

CHAPTER SIX

The Years After Transplant

Life does not instantly return to normal after bone marrow transplant. Dr. Gutman explained it as similar to being a newborn in a new world. In many ways I was a newborn. My body was starting over. My blood DNA was reset as I explained in the last chapter. My new red blood cells, white blood cells, and platelets that were growing now had the DNA of my sister. I don't know if this is just a factor due to the traumatic experience of transplant or related to my sister's blood DNA, but all of sudden, I felt more emotional. I seemed to tear up a lot more when telling my story to others, testifying to God's amazing love, or hearing someone else's story of struggle. My heart was pulled into conversations in an emotional way I had not experienced before. My sister says I'm more emotionally connected with her blood DNA. I'm not sure of the biology of all of that, but I did take notice of the difference, and so did others. Either way, there seems to be a lot that you inherit from your donor.

One thing you don't inherit from your donor, as I was told by my medical team, is their immunities, or immunizations. My long shot record from growing up as an Air Force dependent, cadet, and officer were all gone—they were wiped out with my old bone marrow. I had to start all over with my immunizations. My medical team referred to it as "receiving your baby shots all over again." It was like Day 0 of transplant became my first day in the world. And I would turn one, two, then three years old, and so on from here on out. Sure enough, two years after transplant, I started to receive my baby shots all over again. They were spaced according to a plan between that second and third year after transplant. It felt strange getting all of these shots, but I knew it was for my protection. My immune system had to be tuned back up to fight off disease that still exists in our world.

For the next four years, 2011-2015, my immune system grew and I recovered according to what my medical team had planned for me. Those were years filled with great memories and a desire to put leukemia behind us.

I have to back up a bit here to the end of transplant in 2011. Nearing the end of my stay at Anschutz in April, some close friends of ours—Todd and Barb Anderson—stopped by and visited with me in the hospital. Todd and Barb are a wonderful couple who know how to lean into life, they love and pray fervently, and they are especially intentional in raising their own family. That night we talked about memories and what life would be like after transplant. I had a heavy heart for Jennifer, 22 at the time. Both Debbie and I were very aware of her deep desire to be married and had many conversations with Jennifer about that desire since the time she had graduated from college the year before. I shared her desire with Todd and Barb that night. Todd and Barb gathered around my hospital bed and leaned into a prayer on behalf of Jennifer's desire to be married. It was a bold prayer, asking God to move on Jennifer's behalf and intersect the path of a young man with her life. And that God would move sooner rather than later.

We didn't know it at the time, but back in Colorado Springs, within a few days of this prayer, a young man had noticed Jennifer. Jennifer was attending a dinner group through our church's young adult ministry. We encouraged her to participate in this dinner group knowing that it would give her a break from being alone in the house while we were in Denver. Jennifer was starting to connect with new friends there, including this young man—Andrew. It began with casual conversations, but God was beginning to do something.

It turns out that Andrew was a senior cadet at the Air Force Academy. Jennifer and Andrew first connected about a month before he was to graduate in May 2011. Over the next several weeks they heard each other's stories and became more acquainted. Their conversations happened during the time when we had yet to be released to go back home to Colorado Springs. We could tell by our conversations with Jennifer that this relationship with Andrew was going somewhere. I had always wanted to be intentionally involved in helping Jennifer confirm that God had brought the right man into her life for possibility of marriage. But, here I was up in Denver, with a brand new immune system still vulnerable to diseases and infections. I was told to stay put in the apartment until my doctor released me.

One evening, Debbie received a call on her cell phone from Jennifer. Jennifer said that Andrew had asked her to meet at a park near our house to go on a short hike the next day. She wanted to know if that was ok. Of course, we said yes. Jennifer was old enough to make her own decisions, and she was certainly mature enough to handle such a situation on her own. The next day came, and Debbie received another call from Jennifer in the afternoon. This time Andrew was with her. She said they were walking at the park and wanted both of us on the phone. So, Debbie put the phone on speaker and brought it to me so we could both listen. Once Andrew was on the phone, Debbie and I introduced ourselves and found out a little more about him. After that, Andrew paused, and then said, "I think you have a special daughter. I would like your permission to pursue a relationship with her." We were filled with excitement, and then quickly brought back into the reality that we were stuck in Denver. We had a desire to meet Andrew, but I was not supposed to leave the apartment except to walk over to the hospital for my appointments. We told

Jennifer and Andrew to give us a moment to consider some options and we would call back.

Once off the phone, I looked at Debbie and said, "We have to find a way to meet him—I don't want to miss out on this." I thought of an idea to meet them halfway between Colorado Springs and Denver, in a town called Castle Rock. Maybe we could find a restaurant and meet for dinner that night. I told Debbie, "You drive and I'll be fine. I'll wear a hospital mask. And I'll just drink water—I won't eat any food." I said that because I knew the guidelines my doctor had given me. I always had to have a mask on, even when walking from the apartment over to the hospital for my regular checks, just a couple blocks away. Another guideline was that I had to be careful of the food I ate. It had to be well cooked. And absolutely no salad bars or buffets. We looked up what was convenient and open at that time in Castle Rock, right off the freeway. I looked at my maps program and saw there was an Applebee's and that it was open until 10:00 p.m. that night. We decided that sounded like a safe place to go. So, we called Jennifer back and gave her and Andrew the idea of meeting that evening for dinner. They agreed, and all of us decided on a time to meet, about two hours later.

I was anxious walking into the restaurant. I had not been anywhere in the outside world in almost two months. I was going into a place that we couldn't control. Even touching the door handle made me nervous. It was like having an "obsessive-compulsive disorder" over making sure everything was clean and wiped off. Inside, we met Jennifer and Andrew and were escorted to a table. I just asked for water and so did Debbie. It was late and we already had dinner before we left, knowing that it would not be a good idea to test my immune system at a restaurant where we didn't know the food was cooked. Jennifer and Andrew did order their dinners. So, Debbie and I watched them eat while we engaged in conversation, learning more about Andrew and hearing some of the stories of Andrew and Jennifer getting to know each other over the past few weeks.

The evening ended and it was time to get back to the apartment. The relationship between Jennifer and Andrew felt good. He seemed like a fine young man. I assumed the best about him as an Air Force Academy cadet and future officer in the Air Force. Young men and women go through tough challenges and develop a lot of maturity just going through a place like the Air Force Academy. It's a great experience for any young man, or woman, who want to serve their country. Before leaving, we told Jennifer and Andrew that we were in favor of them pursuing a relationship. We gave them our blessing and prayed over them.

That was a wonderful experience for me. I felt that I was at least somewhat involved in encouraging Jennifer as her father. She didn't have to walk this journey alone. Both Debbie and I approved of the next steps and looked forward to how God would unfold their story together. That story ended up in marriage a year later—a wedding at the Air Force Academy Chapel in May 2012. Jennifer joined Andrew at a base in Mississippi as he finished up pilot training.

Shortly after Jennifer and Andrew's wedding, Debbie and I celebrated our twenty-fifth wedding anniversary and flew to Maui to celebrate. We had a wonderful time celebrating twenty-five years together. If there is a return to normal after battling leukemia in 2010 and 2011, I felt I was there. I was feeling as close to a normal, fully healthy life as Debbie and I went on that trip. We were having fun enjoying walking along beautiful beaches, watching the sunset over the Pacific Ocean, and just taking in some much needed down time.

Brian was just finishing his first year at the Air Force Academy when Jennifer met Andrew in 2011. He was at graduation, sitting with Jennifer, as they watched Andrew graduate. We didn't know it at the time, but God was also working in Brian's life to prepare him for marriage. Just a few months after Jennifer and Andrew were married, Brian took notice of a young lady at an outdoor Christian concert near Ft. Collins, Colorado. It was the Summer of 2012 as Brian was beginning his junior year at the Air Force Academy. In the Fall of 2012, Brian called us and said he wanted us to meet someone special in his life. We decided to meet in Denver for dinner. Brian walked in with a beautiful young woman and introduced Kaitlyn to us. We had a wonderful time getting to know Kaitlyn and hearing the details of how they met. At this Christian concert, the group on stage encouraged the audience to meet those around them and worship together. Kaitlyn introduced herself to Brian. Brian took note of her name, connected on social media, and a few weeks later they met in person. In June 2013, on Kaitlyn's birthday, Brian proposed, Kaitlyn said yes, and they set their wedding date for May 31, 2014—a few days after Brian's graduation from the Air Force Academy.

During that same year, 2013, Jennifer and Andrew announced they were pregnant. Debbie and I would have our first grandchild. We were thrilled for this new chapter in our lives—being grandparents. In November 2013 we welcomed Caleb into our family. Not only was Debbie made to be a wonderful mother, she was made to be a wonderful grandma—God had gifted her with an amazing ability to serve our family with the love of Christ. I enjoyed watching Debbie fulfill that gifting as she so wonderfully loved on Caleb and served Jennifer and Andrew so well anytime we could be with them. It wouldn't be long until we adopted new names so that Caleb would have an easy way to identify Debbie and I. Debbie was called "Mimi" and I was called "Gpa."

Brian's graduation was coming up in May 2014. A few months before graduation, Brian asked if I could commission him into the Air Force. I was deeply honored that he asked. At the Air Force Academy, commissioning is usually held the evening before graduation. This event marks the transition from "officer trainee" to "officer" in the Air Force. The most significant part of the commissioning ceremony is when each cadet takes the commissioning oath and swears "to support and defend the Constitution of the United States." There are more words to the oath, but the essence of it is taking on a weighty responsibility to serve your nation.

So, on the evening of May 27, 2014, I had the privilege of commissioning Brian into the United States Air Force as a Second Lieutenant. I was filled with pride as I read the oath to Brian, we exchanged salutes, and Kaitlyn and Debbie pinned on his new Second Lieutenant rank. The significance of this date is that exactly twenty-seven years before (May 27, 1987), I had graduated from the Air Force Academy. I was full of emotion as I thought back twenty-seven years and remembered all the blessings in my own life, and in the life of our family. Here was my son stepping into significant service of his country. Brian graduated the next day (May 28), and three days later married Kaitlyn at the Air Force Academy (May 31). We were definitely a "blue Air Force" family at that wedding. Andrew, Brian, and I all wore formal Air Force mess dress for Brian's wedding. I loved that moment of our family being together and witnessing the legacy of Air Force service unfold.

As I have tried to describe, the years from 2011-2015 were filled with wonderful news and great memories. Leukemia was starting to become a distant memory. We all were learning to move beyond living with the hardships of cancer, little knowing more health challenges were ahead.

CHAPTER SEVEN

Another Chapter in the Journey

At the end of 2014 and beginning of 2015, I started to experience significant back pain and numbness in my left foot. Based on the symptoms, my doctor was pretty sure I had Sciatica. Sciatica is often caused by a herniated disk or narrowing of the spine that compresses part of the nerve. It often results in numbness along a specific leg. He ordered an MRI scan to see what was going on. A few weeks later I was able to get an MRI and the results showed that I had narrowing of the spine at the two lowest vertebrae in the lumbar area (referred to as spinal stenosis). In addition, I showed symptoms of degenerative disc disease. Degenerative disc disease is caused by wear-and-tear on a spinal disc. It actually is a fairly normal condition as we age—the wear-and-tear on a spinal disc after sixty, seventy, and eighty years of use can start to cause us problems. But I was only 50 years old! Outside of leukemia, I had been pretty healthy and physically active. I never had any back problems.

Shortly after the MRI, I had a follow-up appointment with Dr. Gutman. I asked him about the results of the MRI and the conditions of spinal stenosis and degenerative disc disease. I wanted to know if these conditions had any relationship to leukemia and bone marrow transplant. He did tell me that there can be many side effects of bone marrow transplant. I remember him saying, "We now have an amazing ability to save people's lives through bone marrow transplant, but it often comes with a cost." He told me the treatment I went through with chemo, radiation, and cancer drugs can often weaken the bones, especially the soft, fluid part of the spine—the discs. Cancer treatment can basically accelerate the aging of the spine. In essence, my spine was more like someone in their sixties, seventies, or eighties, rather than someone in their fifties. He recommended that I see a spine surgeon to explore options.

I got connected with a wonderful spine surgeon in Colorado. She confirmed that I had spinal stenosis in L4/L5, the lower part of the lumbar spine. Her recommendation was a laminotomy—essentially a procedure to give the arch in my spinal vertebrae more room and to relieve pressure. She said that a laminotomy is less invasive than other procedures because it removes less bone. This spine surgeon came highly recommended, so I agreed to the surgery. Surgery was scheduled for April 14, 2015 at a spine center near Boulder, Colorado. Debbie and I drove up the night before since we had to be at the spine center early that morning. I was told that I would only be there for part of the day—the surgery would only take an hour and then a few hours to recover. I was amazed that I actually walked out of the spine center about four hours after surgery, with a Velcro back brace, and a little help from Debbie. We got in the car and Debbie drove us home. I couldn't believe I just had back surgery and was home by dinner. Medical breakthroughs have come a long way.

I did have to be careful for about six weeks to make sure I was not lifting anything more than ten pounds and to keep my back relatively straight—no bending over to lift anything. I seemed to recover according to my doctor's plans, and the Sciatica slowly started to disappear.

One morning during the recovery from back surgery, I woke up and noticed a small bump on the right side of my face, slightly behind my eye. It was very painful. I didn't know if this was related to my back surgery or maybe an infection in that area. I took notice of it for a few days and it didn't go away. I decided to go to my primary doctor and see if he could figure out what this was. He thought that maybe I was bitten by something while I was sleeping—possibly a spider bite. He gave me some ointment to put on it and said to watch it to see if it would go away.

Several weeks went by and the bump was still there. It didn't appear to be getting any bigger, but it definitely wasn't going away. I also began noticing some dizziness, mostly when I rotated my head quickly, like when getting up out of bed. It felt like the world was spinning on me for a few seconds. At the end of May 2015, Debbie, Zachary, and I went to visit Jennifer and Andrew in Tacoma, Washington. They were at their second assignment, at McChord Air Force Base. I would often take Zachary and Caleb (now 18 months) up to a playground near their house on base. While walking back with them, I felt some of this dizziness and told the boys I needed to stop for a moment. I grabbed onto a light pole nearby to steady myself. The dizziness quickly went away. This happened a couple more times while we were at Jennifer and Andrew's house. I really didn't think much of it and attributed it to something related to my back surgery.

Near the end of June, I had a final follow-up with my spine surgeon up in Boulder, Colorado. I drove the hour and a half up to that appointment. Debbie and Zachary were with me as I wanted to take them to a fun Mexican restaurant after the appointment. I parked the car at the clinic and we all began walking to the front entrance. As I was walking, I felt the world spin on me and I could tell I was going to go down. I told Debbie, "I'm not feeling well and I think I need to take a knee." I grabbed onto her and she slowly helped me to sit down, right there in the middle of the parking lot. A man nearby saw what was happening and came over to help. Debbie told him that I felt dizzy and was having a hard time walking. He worked at the clinic and went in and got a wheelchair. He brought out a wheelchair and helped me get into the clinic. Once inside I felt fine and told him I was able to stand up and walk the rest of the way to my appointment.

We all sat down in the waiting room and we were all wondering what just happened. *Was this something related to my back surgery?* I remember Debbie saying, "You need to tell the spine surgeon what just happened." That was on my mind also. Debbie and I were called into the doctor's office while Zachary stayed in the waiting room, reading a book. My spine surgeon had me do several tests of bending in different directions and feeling my spine. She said that everything looked great. At the end of those tests, I told her what happened in the parking lot. She took a moment to ask some more questions and then did some tests where she watched my eyes track an object and looked at my eyes with a light. She said, "I don't know what is going on, but you need a brain MRI right away. I am going to write an order for you to get a brain MRI back in Colorado Springs, today."

We were stunned leaving my spine surgeon's office. Was there something going on inside my brain causing this dizziness? We all got in the car at the parking lot and I had Debbie drive, knowing it was probably not wise for me to drive. It was past lunch time, so we decided to find a quick place to eat—not the Mexican restaurant I wanted to take Debbie and Zachary to. A few miles away we found a Chipotle and decided to eat there. We walked in and stood in line to order. While waiting in line, I started to feel dizzy/light-headed again. A woman nearby noticed what was happening as I grabbed a railing to steady myself. She told Debbie she was a nurse from the hospital and would help her escort me to a chair to sit down. I sat down and thanked her for her help. She also told Debbie that my pulse and breathing were normal and that I would be ok. She had assessed my situation that quickly.

After lunch, we got back in the car and Debbie drove us the ninety minutes back to Colorado Springs. Along the way, I called my primary doctor's office and told them what had happened and that we were coming straight to their clinic for an MRI. We also called Debbie's parents so they could meet me at the doctor's office and take Zachary in case we were a long time. The nurses at my doctor's office were expecting us as we arrived. I showed my primary doctor the note my spine surgeon had given me. It said, "Need brain MRI ASAP for syncope." That's the first time I had actually read the note. Syncope is the medical term for fainting or passing out. My primary doctor quickly examined me and said that I would need to go to the emergency room at Memorial Hospital in downtown Colorado Springs. They tried to get me into the MRI clinic next door to their office, but it was booked. My doctor said they called ahead to Memorial and they had a slot open for me.

Since Memorial Hospital was expecting us, we didn't have to wait long in the emergency room. After just a short wait, Debbie and I were escorted to a room. There, a female ER doctor came in to get my vitals and explained what would happen in the MRI room. Shortly after that, I was rolled into the MRI room and prepared for the scan. I had experienced an MRI for diagnosing my back problems, so it all looked familiar. This time, however, they placed my head in a device that would keep my head from moving while they performed the scan. I think the scan took about thirty minutes before I was rolled back to my room. Then we waited for the results.

About an hour went by, and the ER doctor came back with the results of the MRI. We had a growing awareness that something wasn't right. She said I had a massive tumor on the right side of my brain that was also causing the swelled spot on that side of my face. She said the tumor looked like a meningioma—a tumor that forms in the outside layer of your brain. We were stunned—I have a brain tumor! We asked the most obvious next question, "Is this a cancerous tumor?" The ER doctor replied with, "Most meningiomas are non-cancerous. They can often grow slowly over several years without any symptoms. The location of this meningioma is likely causing the syncope symptoms (fainting/passing out) that you are experiencing." I can't even remember what

Debbie and I said to each other. We were stunned and thinking, *here is another medical issue to deal with.* But hearing that this was likely "not cancer" was a relief. *Ok,* I thought, *I can do this.*

The ER doctor recommended that I follow-up with a neurosurgeon she worked with right away. She gave me the name of that neurosurgeon and also prescribed some medicine that would reduce the chances of a seizure. She was concerned about the size of this tumor. It was huge—the size of an orange, and it was placing pressure on my brain. Seizures can be a common side effect, and the doctor wanted to prevent any chances of a seizure. So, I was given the medication and also told I couldn't drive while on this medicine. We left the emergency room late that night, picked up Zachary at Debbie's parents' house, and went home.

We were able to get an appointment with the neurosurgeon about a week later. We met with him to review the brain scan. I remember him telling us that it didn't look like a normal meningioma. It was very complex and extended in a couple different directions. Debbie and I could tell he was very experienced. But it wasn't long before he said that there was someone much better at removing these tumors than he was. This neurosurgeon we were meeting with, and Memorial Hospital where I went to the emergency room, were part of the University of Colorado Health System, the same hospital network where I had the bone marrow transplant—at the Anschutz campus in Denver. He mentioned the name of the best neurosurgeon on their team up in Denver—Dr. A Samy Youssef. He told us he would get in contact with Dr. Youssef so I should see him next.

It was the second week in July 2015 when Debbie and I drove up to Anschutz to see Dr. Youssef. It was a weird feeling being up there again. I had been up there for regular blood checks the last few years since 2015, but not to see a doctor, for a different medical condition. We didn't know what was ahead other than this would require brain surgery. Dr. Youssef was very professional and thorough in his explanation of the tumor. He had a couple residents with him and they watched intently as he interacted with us. He showed us very detailed scans of the tumor, taken at Memorial Hospital the month earlier. And he explained how he expected the surgery to go. He said he would like to remove the tumor sooner, rather than later. Looking at his calendar, he had an open date on July 29, 2015—a little less than three weeks away. The date was set—I was going to have brain surgery.

Debbie and I went up the night before and stayed in a Marriott hotel near Anschutz. A friend of ours from church was so generous and gifted us several hotel rooms for our family to support me in my surgery. Jennifer was in town, and pregnant with our second grandchild. She also joined us while a friend watched Caleb and our own Zachary at home. Brian was in pilot training and flew in to be with us. Debbie's parents were also there to support us. I had my family surround me with love as we prepared for this very serious surgery.

Debbie and I got up early the next morning and walked over to Anschutz. I had to check in at 6:30 a.m. The sun was just coming up as we walked over. I don't know if I really absorbed the heaviness of brain surgery. I was going into this experience like any other surgery I had—I'll get an IV, I'll go to sleep, I'll wake up and it will all be over. That's really what I was feeling as we walked over. I really thought this would be a simple surgery to remove the tumor, and then life would return to normal. But I think others suspected a connection to my previous experiences with cancer.

It took a long time for me to get prepped for surgery. Debbie had cut my hair close (buzz cut) the day before so that the surgical team didn't have to mess with that. I was told they would shave my head even closer in the area around my brain where they were going to be operating. When the medical team took me back for surgery, Debbie walked back to the hotel where Jennifer, Brian, and Debbie's parents were staying. Only Debbie and my family know what the next nine hours looked like.

From Debbie's view ...

At the hotel, we all just tried to pass the time as best we could. I had brought lunch and snacks for everyone. Every few hours I would get a call from a nurse in the operating room on how the surgery was progressing. I think we were told that the surgery would take about 5-6 hours. The surgery actually went beyond that timeframe. I wasn't really worried since the nurse continued to update me on progress. My only concern was that Brian had to leave early that evening to catch a flight back to his pilot training base. Around 3:30 p.m. the nurse called and said the doctor was almost done with surgery and that he wanted to meet with us in about 30 minutes. We all walked over to the hospital at that time. When we got to the surgical waiting room, the nurse called us back to a conference room and Dr. Youssef walked in. He told us that the surgery went well and the surgical team was finishing up. He said, "We tested the tumor and the results were not conclusive as to the type of tumor." They were sending the tumor to the laboratory for further testing and it would take a couple days to learn those results. I mentioned to Dr. Youssef that Brian had to leave soon and asked if it would be possible for Brian to see Terence before he left. Dr. Youssef said he would try to accommodate our request. We all went to the ICU waiting room and waited for further instructions.

The first thing I remember is waking up and saying the word, "nausea." I was feeling really sick as I started to wake up. The nurse with me said he would give more medicine in my IV to help with that. I remember having to say it a couple more times until he gave me enough medicine to make that feeling go away. I've had several surgeries before and never had a problem with nausea. I'm told it was likely due to the heavy medication and the long time I was put under. After the nausea was under control, Dr. Youssef came in and checked on me. He said they had to do a lot of work to remove the tumor, but that he felt good with the outcome. He asked if I wanted to see my family. Of course, I said yes. I was wheeled out to the ICU room and the first person who met me there was Brian. He had to fly out in a few hours, back to pilot training, and wanted to see me before he left. I still can't believe I have a pretty clear memory of that moment. I think it was just a few seconds of interaction. And I said something like this to him, "Go fly jets." That's it—I think that's all I said. I have no memory of what he said that night, just that memory of what I said to him. I really don't have much memory of the rest of the night, but Debbie and Jennifer do since they saw me right after Brian left.

From Jennifer's view…

After Brian left, Mom and I went in to see Dad in ICU. I'm not sure what I expected to see after a brain surgery, but I tried to prepare myself for any outcome. I was stunned by what I saw. My Dad was black and blue around his right eye, and his head was extremely swollen. His head was wrapped in several layers of white gauze and he was lying in a huge bed, with pillows all around him. He had IVs in both arms, and there were monitors and lights beeping and flashing. Dad was able to slowly respond to some questions, but I could tell he felt awful and wasn't fully aware. He was very tired and we knew we couldn't stay long. My Mom and I said goodbye and walked to the hotel across from the hospital, before I drove back to Colorado Springs to pick up Zachary and Caleb, wondering how my Dad would be able to recover from the effects of such extensive surgery.

I remember waking up early the next morning and felt a bit clearer in my mind. I noticed my phone sitting on a tray near my bed and assumed Debbie had put it there the night before. I reached for it and saw there was a text message from our neighbor behind us, Garvin McCarrell. At that time, Garvin was one of the pastors at our church. His text said, "Terence, I took a picture of your house this morning as you were going into surgery. There is a double rainbow over your house right now. You are in good hands. God is with you." I have that picture saved on my phone to remind me of God's closeness that day and I use it to tell my story, and especially the story about how God was already doing something beautiful in the midst of the storm we were going through.

I spent the next three days in ICU recovering from brain surgery. As standard practice for a tumor, my neurosurgeon sent the tumor off for a biopsy and he expected to have the results in a day or so. On the third day, a doctor walked into our room—we had not seen this doctor before. She introduced herself and said she had the results from the biopsy of the tumor. Without much drama or emotion, she said they had found traces of leukemia in the tumor. And then she said, "We will be referring your case to the Bone Marrow Transplant team and we will move you to their floor tomorrow." I was stunned. Leukemia? We were told this was a meningioma—a non-cancerous brain tumor. Why was there talk of bone marrow transplant? The darkness of a third round of fighting leukemia sunk into our hearts. This time, it was in the brain and we felt another difficult and unknown journey was ahead of us.

The next day, I was moved to the eleventh floor of Anschutz—the Bone Marrow Transplant floor. It was surreal going back to the eleventh floor—the same floor I was on during 2011 for transplant. And by God's providence, I was back in the same room that I was in during 2011 for transplant. There I would go through another round of chemo and radiation treatments. The radiation treatments were very targeted to the right frontal lobe of my brain to eliminate any traces of the tumor that could not be removed surgically. I would also receive additional chemo treatments in my spinal fluid. My doctors suspected that a few cells of leukemia were not completely eliminated during bone marrow transplant in 2011, crossed the blood-brain barrier into my spinal fluid, and developed into the tumor over a period of years. The medical team took a sample of my spinal fluid and they did find leukemia in the fluid, confirming that leukemia was not completely wiped out during transplant. My doctors had to take an aggressive approach to make sure the leukemia was completely eliminated from my spinal fluid. Leukemia developing into a solid tumor in the brain was a very rare and catastrophic condition. A large team of doctors met to determine a unique, and mostly experimental, course of treatment. Although we were never told this, Debbie and I could feel that the treatment was a long shot for something so rare.

I spent another three weeks in the hospital after my initial recovery from brain surgery. Most of that time was due to an infection from the first round of chemo, similar to what I experienced in 2010 when my blood counts were low and I developed a fever. I was in the hospital for two straight weeks, just for the infection, as the medical team tried several different antibiotics to try to eliminate the infection. It was during this time that I experienced the most traumatic event of my journey. I was receiving radiation treatments about three times a week while at Anschutz for the infection. My nurse would wheel me down to the radiation oncology unit on the first floor. There, I was placed on a table and my head inserted into a brace to keep it from moving. A large machine (called Gamma Knife) delivered radiation to a very specific part of my brain where the tumor had been located. At the end of this treatment, my nurse would bring me back to my room. On one occasion after getting back to my room, I remember shivering with cold. I asked my nurse for some warm blankets. She placed a blanket over me, but it wasn't enough—I was still freezing. She got some more warm blankets, but I couldn't stop shaking. She left the room and it was just Debbie and I. Whatever was going on in my body must have looked pretty intense from Debbie's view. Debbie shouted out, "Help. Can we get a nurse in here right now—he is not doing well!"

From Debbie's view…

I could tell Terence was struggling. At first, I thought the blankets would help and he would get warmer. But that wasn't happening. When the nurse left, he made a turn for the worse and was shaking uncontrollably. I could tell he needed more help. So, I shouted out for a nurse. A nurse came running back and could also tell that Terence was in some type of shock after his radiation treatment. The nurse quickly called for more help, and the next thing I saw was about ten people rush into his room—doctors and nurses. They were trying different medications in his IV line to try to resolve the reaction he had from radiation. Nothing seemed to be working. I felt so alone. I quickly reached for my phone and texted Terence's best friend, Kevin Dailey, and asked him to pray. And I texted our family and some other friends. One of the doctors I knew well came over to me and said, "Are you doing ok?" I'm not sure of what I told her. In that moment, I thought this was going to be it. Terence looked like he was dying and I was witnessing his last moments. After about an hour of multiple medication attempts, Terence's body started to settle down and warm up. Later, his nurse told us they were not absolutely sure of what happened, but concluded Terence must have had an adverse reaction to the radiation. Terence then had to return to ICU to be more closely watched.

This traumatic event certainly did not hasten my time to get out of the hospital. I was kept in the hospital longer than we originally thought, because of the infection and the intense reaction to radiation treatment. Jennifer was approaching her due date and I could tell Debbie was wrestling with what to do. Both Jennifer and I needed Debbie, but we were in different States—Jennifer in Washington and me in Colorado. About a week after the intense reaction to radiation, I started to get back to normal and wasn't having to be watched as closely. Debbie asked the doctor how I was doing and if it was safe to leave me. He said that I was stable and felt confident that everything was under control for her to leave. So, with much emotion, we made the decision that Debbie needed to be with Jennifer before her due date. Debbie flew out to Washington around the first of September. A few days later, I had an amazing surprise. Brian and his wife Kaitlyn drove in from pilot training in Oklahoma to visit me for Labor Day weekend (September 2015). I remember the nurse opening the door and saying, "Terence, you have some special visitors." Right behind her was Brian and Kaitlyn. I was shocked—I had no idea they were planning to visit me, and it came at such a great time while Debbie was gone. The next day after their visit I was released from the hospital. We all went to Debbie's parents (Bruce and Lynda) house that weekend. I recovered at their home while Debbie was in Washington. A few days later, on September 7, our second grandbaby was born—Eleanor. I was excited and sad at the same time. I was in no condition to travel and recognized it would be a long time before I would see Eleanor.

I remember asking Dr. Youssef at one of my first follow-up appointments how long it would take to recover from this type of brain tumor. I couldn't believe what he said: "Give it two years; you have been through a lot." But I thought, *it won't take me two years. I've been through leukemia and a bone marrow transplant. I'll be back to normal in six months.* I couldn't imagine taking two years to recover from something, even a brain tumor. But, that's exactly how long it took. I did start working a few months later, but it was slow. My mind couldn't think clearly all the time. I had to take short breaks and rest. I couldn't just focus for 8 or 9 hours like I used to. Eventually my strength came back and I could think and focus like I used to. But I could tell I wasn't 100 percent. My long-term memory seemed to be fine—I could remember details from long ago. But my short-term memory was a different story. I could tell it was easy for me to forget things that were told to me a few minutes or hours ago. If I didn't rehearse or write something down, it was gone. At first, it was hard to accept. But *if this is all I have to deal with after brain surgery, I'll accept it. It could have been a lot worse for what I have been through.* So, I pressed on and did the best I could, recognizing that likely my memory would never be quite as sharp due to the trauma I experienced. After about two years, I felt a lot better. I was able to work and contribute to TiER1 with a high level of satisfaction. In fact, the research team I was leading at TiER1 continued to win research grants with the federal government and our business grew. Only by God's grace and miraculous touch on me could this have happened.

CHAPTER EIGHT

The Family Speaks

Debbie's words...

When we received the call that Terence had leukemia, I remember thinking, *why us?* What did we do to deserve this disruption to all of our lives? All of our lives changed so much. My parents moved into our house to help keep us going during that time since I was at the hospital every day, and Zachary needed care. During this initial time in the hospital so many people made us meals and helped us in many ways. Still, it is easy to feel so alone, but we knew that God was with us. I was so thankful that Terence was well enough to be involved in all the graduation activities for Jennifer and Brian. After he completed treatment in the Fall of 2010, we moved on with our lives because we were told Terence had a very treatable form of leukemia and was cured.

When Terence relapsed in 2011, it was hard to believe because he didn't look or feel sick—his doctor had caught the leukemia at a much earlier point. As soon as we learned Terence would have to be up in Denver for an extended time for transplant, we talked through what each of us would need to make it through bone marrow transplant and the extended stay in Denver. Terence wanted me to still be able to visit him frequently, and I didn't want to have to leave Zachary in Colorado Springs, so my parents moved with us to Denver to be able to help with him once again. Jennifer and Brian were both now established in their lives, so we were only able to see them when they could work it out. As a mother I knew they were both adults and they would be fine on their own, but I also felt God was asking me to once again give both Jennifer and Brian to God's care and trust Him to work in their lives. I had to believe that He loves them both more than I ever could.

I remember the day before the transplant was to take place in Denver; it was beautiful outside and Terence was really struggling with why he had to go through all of this when he seemed to feel fine. Zachary was not going to be able to see Terence for 30 days during transplant because children were not allowed on the bone marrow transplant floor. Before transplant, Terence wrote in his journal and prayed that he would live to see Brian graduate from the Air Force Academy and to walk Jennifer down the aisle someday. This second time around God helped me realize how much I needed Him and He gave me such amazing peace. I remember the very anticlimactic moment on the evening Terence received the transplant, April 11th, 2011, when the bag of bone marrow was delivered to Terence's room from his sister, Bonita. The doctors were amazed how well Terence did given the circumstances, and Terence ended up being released on my birthday, April 29th. After a few setbacks, once again Terence was given a very confident report that he had come through miraculously and he could go on with his life.

While we were in Denver, Jennifer met Andrew and was married a year later in 2012. Once again God answered prayer and Terence got to walk her down the aisle on May 5, 2012. Terence and I celebrated our twenty-fifth wedding anniversary on May 30, 2012 in Maui, Hawaii. Brian graduated from the Air Force Academy on May 28, 2014 and then married a wonderful young lady, Kaitlyn, three days later on May 31st. Zachary was growing up and continued to be a joy to our lives.

Caleb Philip Lee, our first grandchild, was born on November 11, 2013 and added so much excitement for all of us. Our life once again seemed very much back to normal.

When the brain tumor was discovered in 2015, it felt like another setback. I had lots of questions about what God was doing, but I knew from 2010 and 2011 that by running to God, I would find His comfort and peace. In the midst of this very dark valley, God blessed our family with a second grandchild, Eleanor Lynn Lee on September 7, 2015. It was so wonderful to experience such an amazing gift from God in the midst of a very difficult time. Terence's recovery from the brain tumor has been very long and challenging. We don't know what will happen next. Sometimes it is hard to dream again because we don't know if our journey through leukemia is forever over.

When we found out about leukemia coming back in Terence's brain, we felt that this third round of cancer was not only for our spiritual growth, but for those around us. The brain tumor treatment and recovery has been much more difficult on Zachary. It is hard to understand why he should have to deal with such big issues at a young age. I've prayed that he will not be bitter with God, but instead he will see God through all that is going on. During the days of Terence's recovery and treatments during 2015, I spent a lot of time reading the book of Psalms. I wanted to find a way to praise even when things were hard. David writes a lot about enduring hard times in the book of Psalms. Each time the leukemia has come back it has been progressively more serious and has caused us to lean into God even more. I recently listened to a talk that the late Elisabeth Elliot gave in which she talks about suffering. Hebrews 5:8 says, "Son though he was, he learned obedience from what he suffered." This verse is talking about Jesus and that He had to suffer to learn obedience. Mrs. Elliot says, "In the gift of suffering God gives himself to me."[7] She also said, "When we don't understand, just bow before a mysterious God."[1] It may not make sense why we would have to suffer, but I know that when life doesn't throw as many hard things in my path, it is easy to grow self-centered and think I don't need to rely on God as much as I should. In the midst of the worst days of watching Terence suffer, I discovered a real presence of God and that He gave me such an amazing peace.

In reflecting over the last eight years I can look back and say, "Why not us?" God wants to give our family a special gift, if we choose to accept it. He has given us the chance to get to know His amazing love and care in a very real way. I have a yearning for Him like I've never known in all the years before 2010. I know that heaven is real and happiness is only forever in heaven.

It is incredible to see Terence able to work and contribute at such a high level at TiER1. After all he has been through I know that it is a miracle he is able to do his job again, and enjoy it. During the bone marrow transplant we read the book of Job and even now I pray Job 42:12 for Terence: "The Lord blessed the latter part of Job's life more than the former part..." I'm looking forward to what God has for us even if the blessings don't look like what I would think best. I have faith to know that "God works for the good of those who love him, who have been called according to His purpose" (Romans 8:28). And this verse in Proverbs has kept me close to God as I have trusted in Him:

> "Trust in the Lord with all your heart
> and lean not on your own
> understanding. In all your ways
> acknowledge him, and He will make
> your paths straight." (Proverbs 3:5-6)

Jennifer's words...

Cancer was always something other people had, something I couldn't imagine dealing with inside my own family. I was 20 years old when my Dad was diagnosed with leukemia the first time, 21 the second time, and 25 the third time. My years of young adulthood ended up being defined by cancer and the resulting tests on my faith. I remember so clearly where I was each time we received news of my Dad's cancer, and each time I had to wrestle with my own belief in God's goodness. I asked the hard questions I'd never considered to that level before—Why, God? How can a good God allow this to happen? Is God really real? Is He punishing me? Those questions still come, but this journey certainly matured me and provided so many opportunities for God to show me His love and care. My Dad tells about feeling God's amazing love very tangibly in a way that overwhelmed him with its force. For me, God's love has slowly grown in my heart as I've seen the quiet miracles along the way.

In 2011, I had just returned home from having tea with a friend when my parents shared that my Dad's cancer had returned. I was devastated. I couldn't believe that after the amazing healing my Dad had experienced, we were again facing this daunting disease. We found out about the relapse around Valentine's Day, and because my parents didn't want to leave me and Zachary, who was 4 years old at the time, we all went out for a nice Valentine's Day dinner together—all trying to enjoy our time, but our hearts were heavy with what we knew was ahead. My parents moved to Denver with Zachary and my grandparents, and I remained in Colorado Springs, teaching Eighth Grade English and visiting Denver on the weekends. It was a lonely journey for me, as many of my friends had married or moved away. I too longed to find community and marriage. A dear mentor of mine challenged me with a promise from Psalm 84:6: "When they walk through the Valley of Weeping, it will become a place of refreshing springs..." (NLT). I prayed to find the joys amidst the sorrow, and I especially prayed that my Dad would live to walk me down the aisle.

In the midst of spending the weeks living alone in my parents' house, I joined a dinner small group through the college ministry at New Life Church. There, in May 2011 as my Dad was recovering from the bone marrow transplant, I met a young man named Andrew... We began to talk over doing dishes and playing games with friends, and just before his graduation from the Air Force Academy, he asked me to begin a relationship with him. My parents drove down from the hospital to meet us that evening and give their blessing—my Dad in a baseball cap and hospital mask. Despite the difficulty of that season, God faithfully answered so many of my prayers, showing me that blessing can come from the valley of weeping. In November, Andrew asked me to marry him, and we were married almost exactly one year after we first met. My Dad walked me down the aisle as the organist played "Praise to the Lord, the Almighty, the King of Creation... Hast thou not seen / How thy desires all have been / Granted in what He ordaineth?"[2] I'm so grateful God has allowed my Dad to remain an important part of my life, and especially as I've watched him become a Gpa to my children.

I was pregnant with our second child, Eleanor, when my parents called to share the news of his brain tumor with my husband and me. I remember us all deciding that we would choose to continue on, choosing to see each day as a gift no matter what happened. God had shown us His faithfulness, and He would provide. We went ahead with Eleanor's baby shower, just a few weeks before my Dad's brain surgery, and I was able to stay in town for the surgery. The strength of God was so strong during it all, but the shock of seeing my Dad just after surgery was stunning. Once we found out that the tumor was indeed a cancer relapse, we all knew the chances of survival weren't good. Before I flew home to Washington to wait for Eleanor's birth, I went in to tell my Dad goodbye. I don't remember all he or I said, but I really thought I was saying goodbye for the last time, even though I so desperately prayed he would live to meet Eleanor. And again, God answered that prayer. Eleanor's name means "shining light of Christ," and through that difficult season, and still now, she's brought so much joy—another evidence of God's love even through the trials of life.

I've seen another glimpse of God's hand at work in my Dad's story and in my own when I was diagnosed in 2017 with a pituitary tumor, and my Dad referred me to his own neurosurgeon, Dr. Youssef, since I was facing the possibility of surgery to remove the tumor. When I was diagnosed, we were told more children may not be possible, but in August 2018, my husband and I left Anschutz hospital in Denver with our little William Scott. I never imagined back in 2011 and 2015 when my Dad spent days and months in the hospital in Denver that I'd be leaving that same hospital with a precious miracle baby. Little William Scott shares my Dad's middle name, and I think it's a fitting testament to God's faithfulness in our family. I pray William will demonstrate the same trust in the Lord that my Dad has lived out before me my whole life.

We don't know what's ahead, but God has truly been faithful in our family. He has answered so many prayers, sometimes not always how we expected, but He's always been present, showing His amazing love.

Brian's words...

As I write this, it has been 8 years since our family met in our basement to find out the news that my Dad had leukemia. When I think back on that time, I realize now more than anything the difficulty and hardship that my mom experienced as much as my Dad. My parents have done an amazing job of having a godly example of marriage, and the past 8 years I saw that manifest more than ever. I am thankful for both of them, and especially the time my Dad was granted to experience many once-in-a-lifetime events like graduations, weddings, and grandchildren. All of these events did not seem guaranteed at many points along this long road.

My Dad's first treatment of leukemia was the only one that I was able to really be present for the entire duration. It showed me a side of him, and our family, that I really hadn't seen before. Growing up we had our share of problems, but to be completely honest, everything seemed relatively simple, and I had never seen my Dad so weak and broken. The next few years passed, and I saw my Dad continue to battle through leukemia, although I was rarely able to visit my family up in Denver due to my schedule at the Air Force Academy. I felt somewhat out of touch with what was going on the during this time. I saw my Dad struggle in ways that were difficult to watch, both physically and mentally. Through that struggle, I saw my Dad grow spiritually like never before. Psalm 3 represented what I saw my Dad endure and overcome over many difficult years of sickness. I saw him cry out to the Lord in pain and be given the strength so that he can now bring that same strength to others through their trials.

> "But you, Lord, are a shield around me,
>
> my glory, the One who lifts my head
>
> high. I call out to the Lord, and he
>
> answers me from his holy mountain. I
>
> lie down and sleep; I wake again
>
> because the Lord sustains me. I will not
>
> fear though tens of thousands assail me
>
> on every side. Arise, Lord! Deliver me,
>
> my God!" (Psalm 3:4-7)

In 2015, I saw my Dad survive an extremely scary brain surgery, and although he doesn't remember very much from that visit, it was just as valuable for me to see him after that surgery as it was for him. Although he looked terrible, having long incisions around his eye and forehead where they had extracted the tumor, I was honored that he made the time for me after such an intense surgery. Despite the long road of recovery that was ahead, when I saw him come out of that surgery I knew he would be ok. It was difficult stepping out and hurrying to the airport and going back to an intense schedule of pilot training the very next day. In my mind I knew that such a surgery would have a very long recovery where I would not be present, and the rest of my family would have to work through the ups and downs over the coming years.

The most difficult part of the whole process for me to watch was the multiple relapses my Dad experienced over a 5-year period. Every time, either sitting down as a family or over the phone, all hope just seemed to be lost as it seemed remission would never be permanent. Thankfully, the prayers of thousands were heard, and I saw many amazing people come together as a result.

All of this brings me back to one passage: "The Lord God said, 'It is not good for the man to be alone. I will make a helper suitable for him'" (Genesis 2:18). At this point God is talking about making Adam a partner, hence Eve, but I believe this also proves our dependence on relationships with others. When a man feels alone and abandoned by God, family, and friends that is when depression and mental illness becomes a serious reality. The people that were, and still are, there for our entire family were perfect examples of how the Body of Christ should respond to those in need. Through trials and tribulations, it is very difficult for anyone to still see God, and I saw my Dad struggle with that, but I also always saw him come back to his faith. I saw my Dad cry out many times asking God where he was and why he was going through this and I struggled with the same questions. This struggle brought me back to a poem I remember reading in a picture frame on a wall by Mary Stevenson called *Footprints in the Sand*. The last line of the poem reads: "Why, when I needed you most, you have not been there for me? The Lord replied, the times when you have seen only one set of footprints, is when I carried you."[3] I know that my Dad genuinely learned that he is, and always has been, loved and carried by the Lord and that is why we should all strive to be amazed by His love.

Zachary's words...

I can remember very clearly when I, my Dad, and my Mom went up to Boulder, Colorado to my Dad's follow-up appointment following back surgery. I noticed my Dad wasn't "normal." When he got out, he walked a few steps and then sat down. I also remember going to Chipotle for lunch after that appointment and my Dad had to sit down as he was feeling light-headed again. If you have read the book (and didn't skip chapter 7!) you will know the story of my Dad's brain tumor.

TERENCE ANDRE

In the car I thought, *what is going on? My Dad has fallen twice. This must be something serious.* I didn't know what was happening to him. I was too young to understand how sick he really was. I just thought it was something a doctor could quickly take care of. When I saw him after he got home from brain surgery, I could tell he was very weak. I remember praying, "help my Dad recover quickly and get well." I am thankful that my Dad has made it through this experience and is still here today to watch me grow up.

CHAPTER NINE

A Company Called TiER1

My story would not be complete without telling about an amazing organization who supported me during my journey through leukemia, bone marrow transplant, and brain tumor. Not many people get to work for a great company that really puts people first, but that is my experience of working for TiER1 Performance Solutions.

I retired from the Air Force in 2007. I was on the faculty at the Air Force Academy at the time. It was the right time to transition out—I had started my journey at the Air Force Academy in 1982 and I finished it in 2007, twenty-five years later, at the Air Force Academy.

Not long after I retired, I was offered a dream job with a small business government contractor. I was going to be their director at a new office they were opening in Dayton, Ohio. I really didn't want to move from Colorado Springs to Dayton, but the job was a perfect match for my experience and skills. I was having a hard time finding something in the Colorado Springs area that fit my background. So, I leaned into taking the job. In the back of my mind I was thinking, *I can do this for a few years and then move back to Colorado Springs when something opens up*.

I began the job working from Colorado Springs until it was time to move to Dayton to open the new office. About a week before I was supposed to travel to Dayton and open the office, Debbie sat down and talked to me about the move. Her first question stopped me in my tracks. She said, "Why are we moving to Dayton, Ohio? We aren't in the Air Force any longer...we can live anywhere we want to live...and we love it here in Colorado Springs. Plus, our children are doing well and we have family here. Do we really have to move to Dayton?" Wow, I was stunned. For some reason I just thought I was supposed to take this job and move to Dayton. We had moved six other times in the Air Force, and I thought, *this is just one more move—we've done this plenty of times.* But, her question hit deep. It made me pause and really think about what I was doing and what my long-term goals were. After taking some time to think about her question, I realized my long-term goal was to stay in Colorado Springs. It's a beautiful area, our friends were here, and Debbie's parents were here. I then talked with Jennifer and Brian, and I could tell they really wanted to stay. They too, were tired of moving. They were in their high school years and were in great school programs at the time. It didn't take me long, maybe a day, before I realized I couldn't take this job in Dayton after all. One of the hardest calls I had to make in my life was calling the president of the company—a man I had known for a long time—and telling him I was not going to continue with the move. I was barely thirty days into the job, and here I was already quitting. I had never done anything like that before; I was always taught to finish what you started. But, I knew I couldn't take this job and move my family across the country. So, that was it—I let my dream job slip away.

I didn't have any backup plans, so I had to start the process of looking for a job all over again, here in Colorado Springs. I had a friend who owned a small consulting business in my field—human factors engineering—and I reached out to him. He had some work coming up where he felt my skills would be useful. So, I waited. Less than a week later I got a call from a friend and former colleague at the Air Force Academy—Daryl Smith. I don't even know how Daryl found my phone number—I had not heard from Daryl in three years. He had retired from the Air Force in 2004, three years before me, and moved back to Northern Kentucky. We had overlapped on the faculty at the Air Force Academy, and he was a wonderful Christian friend. After catching up a bit, Daryl asked, "What are you up to right now?" I told Daryl that I had just quit a job and was on my own for the time being—I didn't have a lot going on. Daryl then said, "This could be really good timing then, I have something to run by you. Can you get on a plane to Cedar Rapids, Iowa in two days and help me facilitate a leadership class at Rockwell Collins?"

I was shocked. I was thinking, *how could I get travel arrangements that quickly, and how was I going to help Daryl with a class I had never seen?* Daryl told me he was working as a contractor for a company named TiER1 Performance Solutions. TiER1 was a small company at that time (less than twenty-five people) based near Daryl's hometown in Covington, Kentucky. He had met the founders of the company (Greg Harmeyer, Norm Desmarais, and Kevin Moore) a few years earlier and came on board as a contractor to help facilitate a leadership class that Kevin was teaching at the time. He had high praise for TiER1 and said I would enjoy facilitating this class with him. So, I agreed.

A few days later I flew to Cedar Rapids and helped Daryl deliver this leadership class to mid-level managers and engineers at Rockwell Collins. Daryl did all the work and gave me prompts ahead of time on how I could help with specific activities within the class. I was mostly there to observe and help out where it made sense. I did enjoy it. It felt good to be teaching again. And Daryl was a pro at interacting with those attending the class. The class was conducted over a 3-day period. After the class finished, Daryl and I said goodbye, and I thought that would be it. But just a few weeks later, Daryl called again and asked if I would be interested in teaching more classes with him. Of course, I said yes! So, over the next few months I started teaching leadership classes about once a month at various Rockwell Collins sites around the country (Cedar Rapids, IA; Melbourne, FL; Los Angeles, CA; and Dallas, TX). It was a lot of fun.

I began teaching with Daryl in November 2007. In December 2007, a friend of mine gave me a tip that a research director position was opening up at the Air Force Academy and suggested that it might be a good fit for me. Even though I was enjoying the teaching with Daryl at TiER1 as a contractor, it was only part-time (about once a month). I desired to have a more consistent, full-time schedule. So, I applied for the job and was called for an interview about a month later in January 2008. I knew several people in the interview session since it was only a few months prior when I was on the faculty at the Air Force Academy. I felt comfortable in the interview, since I knew most of the people asking me questions and digging into my background. I finished the interview and thanked the panel for inviting me and for their interest. Even though I felt I had the skills for the job, I just wasn't sure if they were looking for someone like me who had recently retired, or if they wanted someone who could bring a fresh perspective to this job.

A few weeks went by, and I received a call from the director that I was selected for the job. I felt my spirits lift. Here was an opportunity to stay in Colorado Springs and return to the Air Force Academy. I could keep my family in Colorado Springs. My prayers were answered, I thought. The director who called me said he would turn my hiring package over to Civilian Personnel (equivalent to HR in private industry) and they would contact me when it was time to start the job.

I continued teaching with Daryl as a contractor for TiER1 over the next several weeks. Week after week went by and I had not heard from Civilian Personnel. I was starting to teach more frequently with Daryl and becoming quite familiar with the class. And I was really enjoying it. Two months went by, and I still had not heard from the Academy. It was March

2008. I received a call from Kevin Moore, one of the founders of TiER1, and also one of the facilitators of the class for Rockwell Collins. Kevin would often teach the Rockwell class with Daryl. In fact, it was a question from Kevin that had started this chain reaction of events. Kevin had asked Daryl if he knew any more good people that could join the TiER1 team. Daryl thought of me. Kevin asked if I was available to teach the class with him in a few weeks in Melbourne, FL. I jumped at the chance—I had not met Kevin Moore, but Daryl had told me so much about him. So, I made plans to meet Kevin a few weeks later in Melbourne.

On the afternoon before the class started, I went downstairs to meet Kevin Moore in the conference room where we would teach the class together. We had not met before, but we seemed to find each other without a problem since no one else was in the conference room at that time. Immediately, I could tell Kevin had a great personality and he made it easy to jump into a conversation. The class began that evening with a dinner in the conference room. Kevin handled the introductions and got the participants working in groups at their tables on a few questions that we would use the next day. Kevin and I talked about how the next day would go and who would do what. He also surprised me when he told me he would have to leave in the morning after kicking off the class and drive up to Orlando to give a presentation. He said he would be back during the lunch break. I was a bit stunned. I would need to lead the morning content. Up to this point, I had mostly watched Daryl teach that part—I wasn't sure I was ready to go solo. I remember praying, "Lord, I need some help to get through this—help me remember how Daryl would teach this part." To my surprise, I got through it, although I was eager for Kevin to get back. He did get back near the end of the lunch break so he could take over the afternoon session. Kevin told me later that he could tell I had it all under control. And years later Kevin told me it was that moment in Melbourne when he knew I needed to be with TiER1.

I really enjoyed teaching with Kevin. I could tell Kevin was an excellent teacher. He knew how to make connections in the class and to ask the right questions to get participants engaged. We wrapped up the class the next evening. We couldn't get flights out that night, so Kevin and I stayed one more night. That evening Kevin wanted to take me to his favorite restaurant in Melbourne—a restaurant on the beach with a beautiful setting. After dinner, Kevin said, "You've come all the way to Melbourne, the Atlantic Ocean is right there, let's go touch it." At first I thought it was a little silly—*I've seen the Atlantic Ocean before, why do I need to go touch it?* But I went ahead and walked out on the beach with Kevin, and we touched the ocean. Kevin asked me, "Terence, what is your big dream in life?" I told Kevin that after retirement from the Air Force, my dream was to lead and grow a research team with a small company. I didn't want to be with a large defense contractor, which is quite common for those who retire or transition out of the military. Those companies are just too big; it's hard to feel the impact you are making. I wanted to be a part of something small but growing, something where I could see the tangible outcomes of making an impact. Without hesitating, Kevin said, "TiER1 is small, you should come work with us and build a research team." I would later learn this was quite common for Kevin. He went for the big idea all the time—he wasn't held back by the downsides of an idea. He leaned into dreaming big. I told Kevin I would like to learn more about the company before I could make a decision like that. In the back of my mind, I was thinking that "small" to me was a company of fifty or one hundred people. I had learned that TiER1 was really small—about twenty-three people. I had some concerns about working for a company that small. And my biggest concern was that they were located in Covington, Kentucky. I hardly knew where Covington was located, and I certainly didn't know anyone there other than Daryl.

As we drove back to the hotel, Kevin put a plan in front of me. He said, "I'm going to talk with Greg and Norm about this idea, and I want you to come out and meet them." In response, I told Kevin about the Air Force Academy opportunity. About how it felt like a good opportunity to return to a place I loved, helping the Academy grow a research capability. I also told him that there had been quite a delay—two months had gone by since they told me I was selected in January 2008. Kevin responded, "That's ridiculous, no one should take two months to make a job offer." And then he asked me another direct question. He said, "Are you sure you want to go back to the Air Force Academy? You've already been there and done that. I know it's a cool place, but it's the government. They don't give you much freedom to really do what you want to do." Then Kevin hit me with this idea: "You can't dream big at the Air Force Academy, but you can dream big at TiER1."

We got back to the hotel. As we were getting ready to go back to our rooms, Kevin said, "I'll set this up with Greg and Norm and I'll see you next in Covington." Something else I would learn about Kevin is that he was always much further down the road than everyone else. He was often thinking about taking the next big step, no hesitation. I told Kevin I needed some time to think about it and would call him in a few days. We said our goodbyes, went back to our rooms, and caught our flights out the next morning.

Kevin certainly gave me a lot to think about over the next few days. Before this trip, I was settled on returning to the Air Force Academy. It was the safe option. It was secure. Working for the government is one of the most secure jobs you can have. It doesn't have a lot of upside, but there is very little risk of a downside, like layoffs. As I was praying over this decision to go out and meet the owners of TiER1, I started to hear God say to me, "Terence, why are you so focused on safety and security? Don't you think you can trust me for that? With me you can go after your big dreams. I'll be with you." I was somewhat surprised I was sensing this impression from God to possibly abandon the secure idea and go with something risky. But over the next few days I felt my heart move in the direction of the TiER1 idea, and the Air Force Academy opportunity didn't seem as glamorous. I was really enjoying my time as a contractor for TiER1, and teaching with Daryl, and now Kevin. But I didn't know much about the rest of the company. I needed to know more before I could make a decision. I called Kevin back and said I would be interested in coming out to Covington. Kevin said, "Great, I've already got it set up for the first week in April with Greg and Norm." Again, Kevin was already way down the road.

I booked my flight for a trip out to Covington the first week in April 2008. The day came when I was to fly to Covington. On the way to the airport, I saw a call come in on my cell phone. I recognized it as an Air Force Academy number. I answered it and a lady on the other end said, "Dr Andre, I have your package for the research director position. I need you to come in and sign some forms." I paused for a moment and then said, "I'm on my way out of town, I'll have to do this when I come back." I gave her the date I would be back and told her I would call to make an appointment. I caught my flight to Covington that evening and prepared for my meeting with Greg, Kevin, and Norm the next day.

At that time, TiER1 was located in a historic building in downtown Covington. I took a taxi to their building and found my way to their office on the third floor. There, I met Dee Goodpaster. I would find out later on that Dee was really the "Mom of TiER1"—she took care of every detail. Dee showed me to Kevin's office, and then Kevin took me to a conference room to meet Greg and Norm. The meeting really didn't feel like an interview. Kevin gave some background and then Greg and Norm wanted to hear my story, my aspirations. I used an analogy of green, yellow, and red lights to share my passions. I think we were together for a couple of hours. I felt very comfortable with all three of them. Kevin even mentioned to Greg and Norm that I had an offer to go back to the Air Force Academy and they would have to move quickly if a role at TiER1 was even possible. I ended by telling Greg, Kevin, and Norm that there was one non-negotiable. That non-negotiable was that I had to stay in Colorado Springs. I told them the story of walking away from a job in Dayton, Ohio, and I wasn't going to put my family through that again. Kevin answered with this statement: "We don't care where you live as long as you stand up a research capability and grow it. You can run it from Colorado Springs." I needed to hear that. We wrapped up our time, and Kevin showed me around the office and he introduced me to everyone else who was there. I caught a flight out that night back to Colorado Springs.

On the way back, I could tell my heart was growing more attached to the TiER1 idea. I loved everything about the company. The people I met were extremely talented and I could tell they loved the mission and values of TIER1. And my concern with a possible move was resolved—I could stay put in Colorado Springs. In my morning devotional time the next several days, I felt God moving me to take a step toward TiER1. But, I didn't know if they really wanted me. That question was answered a few days later when Greg emailed an offer to me to come on board the next month—June 2008. I could sense the tension with this decision. The tension between the safe, secure option at the Air Force Academy and the risky option with TiER1. To turn down the Air Force Academy would be tough on me personally. Several of my former colleagues were excited for me to come back. Down deep, I felt that this new, risky journey is what God had designed for me. So, I made my second hardest phone call to tell the Air Force Academy I wasn't taking the job. In less than six months, I had turned down two dream jobs.

I came on board with TiER1 in June 2008. The next month I went back to Covington, Kentucky for my onboarding with the company. TiER1 was having what they called their first "All Company Meeting." Except for a couple people who worked out of their homes a few hours away from Covington, I was the farthest away—out in Colorado. So, it was not hard to bring everyone together. I showed up to the meeting and found out that we were all going to get to know each other better through an "Amazing Race" style event. We were assigned to teams of about five people and given several clues to find across the Covington and Cincinnati areas. Cincinnati is just across the Ohio River from Covington. It was a blast. And it was a cool way to get to know the team at TiER1, and learn some trivia about specific sites around Covington and Cincinnati.

I left that onboarding/amazing race experience with this thought: *Wow, this is a fun company. The Air Force doesn't do things like this. I think I joined the right company.* I continued to teach with Daryl and Kevin over the next few months and started putting some research proposals together for federal grants, especially the Air Force, which I had the most experience with. Then, something dramatic happened. The economy crashed in the Fall of 2008—the beginning of the Great Recession. Within the next few weeks, TiER1 would lose nearly half of their contracts with large companies like Cintas and FedEx. And Rockwell reduced the number of courses they were going to offer in the coming year—courses I was teaching. It was a scary time for the business world. TiER1 was under extreme financial stress, just like every other business. I had never seen this much fear in the economy. Then this thought hit me: *I just made the first major decision in my post-Air Force career and I messed it up. I was the last one in at TiER1 before the economy tanked and I should be the first one out. Shoot, I should have taken the job with the Air Force Academy.* That's exactly what went through my mind. I just assumed TiER1 would have to lay off several people, and I would likely be the first one. But, that didn't happen.

I would learn through this experience what made TiER1 special. Everyone in the company felt the financial stress and the impossible situation we were in. One-by-one, the employees at TIER1 went to Greg, Kevin, and Norm with an idea to weather this storm. Everyone wanted to take significant pay cuts and give up their paid time off. Greg, Kevin, and Norm were overwhelmed by the sacrifice people were willing to make. In the end, Greg, Kevin, and Norm made a decision: "This is the team we want on the other side of this storm. Let's get through this with pay cuts and no paid vacation." So, TiER1 went into survival mode. And I was included in that survival team—I was not laid off. TiER1 did this for about the next year.

One of the values that TIER1 has is placing high value on relationships—the relationships we have with our customers and the relationships we have with each other. I've often said it this way, "Everything flows through relationships." Kevin Moore often says, "So much is accomplished through relationships." That high value placed on relationships would eventually lead TiER1 out of the financial crisis. In just under a year, many of the customers who had to cancel our contracts because of the financial crisis were the first to call us back in to help them rebuild and get their companies back up and running. TiER1 started to grow again, gaining back existing customers and finding new customers. That growth would continue to this day—ten years later. I was significantly impacted by what happened in 2008 and will never be the same. It taught me that the safe route is not always what God wants for us. Sometimes He wants to take us into risky territory, where He can grow and strengthen us, where we can learn. And I learned about leadership as I watched Greg, Kevin, and Norm navigate a very difficult time in the company's history. They did not choose the easy route, the route nearly every other business was choosing. That route was to lay off employees to weather the storm. They kept the team together, sacrificed together, and saw their way to the other side.

That would not be the last challenge TiER1 would face. The next one was with me in February 2010. I've already shared that story in Chapter 2. After receiving the call on a Saturday night, I texted Greg, Kevin, and Norm that I needed to talk with them the next day. I set up a conference call the next day, on Sunday afternoon. On that call, I gave them the background of what just happened and that I would need to be in the hospital for at least the next 30 days. I remember from that call that none of them freaked out. They were calm in their response. They asked me what support I needed and who should take on my responsibilities. And then Kevin said, "We will find a way to get through this." It was an encouraging call. I felt released to focus on this battle and they would do whatever they could to keep the research team moving forward. Years later, Kevin would tell me that after the call he, Greg, and Norm sat in stunned silence for about 15 minutes. TiER1 is a company that solves problems, but in this one, they felt lost. Kevin also told me that in their discussions after I called, they realized that their problem wasn't the leukemia, the problem was taking care of me and my family as best they could. And that's what they did.

A really cool thing happened about one week into my hospital stay. A large box was delivered to my room from TiER1. We opened the box and inside was a Sony DVD player, thirty DVDs, and a fleece blanket from the University of Kentucky—it was March Madness 2010. Inside the sleeve of each movie was a note from a specific person at TiER1 with some background on the movie and why this was their favorite movie. Each person wrote encouraging words for the journey ahead. All of my family were there that morning to open the box. Brian and Zachary took charge of going through the box, reading off the movie titles, and connecting up the Sony DVD player. As I was looking at Brian, Zachary, and Jennifer, I imagined what they were thinking: *Wow, this is pretty cool—Dad being in the hospital has its rewards.* I have no idea if that is what they were actually thinking, but the smiles on their faces were a gift despite the hard days ahead.

As you know from the story in Chapter 2, that would not be the end of the battle with leukemia. It returned in 2011 and I needed a bone marrow transplant. Before my sister was found to be a match, my medical team prepared to go out to the national network to see if someone's blood DNA would be a match for me. While my medical team was preparing to research the bone marrow donor registry, Kevin Moore and another colleague—Rod Ford—came up with an idea. Kevin and Rod knew that all of TiER1 would want to be involved in trying to save my life. They both thought it would be really cool if someone at TiER1 could be selected as my donor if enough characteristics of their DNA were close enough for a match. They did some research and came across Be The

Match©, managed by the National Marrow Donor Program® (NMDP)—the largest marrow registry in the world. Kevin and Rod contacted Be The Match, ordered test kits, and sent emails with links to everyone in the company. In just a few days, TiER1 registered over one hundred people, including spouses. As you already know from Chapter 2, my sister ended up being a perfect match for me—I didn't need to find a donor in the national network. But the TiER1 message to me would be forever etched in my memory—we value you and want to do everything we can to support you.

There would be a third time TiER1 would step up to help me with my battle with leukemia. That was when leukemia came back in the form of a brain tumor in 2015. I was back up at the Anschutz campus in Denver again. By this time, TiER1 had a Denver office and two of my colleagues provided such great support, especially for Debbie. Lissa Burkholder, our Denver business director, came over to the hospital several times to visit and take Debbie for a walk. She even brought smoothies for me as a treat. It was a nice break from the hospital food that could get very routine. Another colleague, Rita Mann, lived just a couple miles from the hospital. She offered an extra room for Debbie. It was such a wonderful gift for Debbie to be able to stay up near the hospital and not drive all the way back to Colorado Springs. Even though it was a small TiER1 team in Denver at the time, it was great not to feel so alone.

I don't know how I ended up being so blessed to work for a great company. A company that not only talks about putting people first, they actually live it out. TiER1 is a special place. I've known for a long time that I worked for a great company. That greatness was recognized in 2017 by Inc. Magazine selecting TiER1 as one of the best workplaces in the United States.[4] That was a huge honor for our company, and I love being able to back up my belief that I work for a great company with this national recognition.

Over the last ten years, I've probably had hundreds of conversations with people about their jobs. Some are classmates from the Air Force Academy. Others are people in my network. And many are from the local community, mainly working for the government or defense contractors. I rarely come across someone who loves everything about their job. It's just not common to hear someone say, "I love everything about my company, the people, and the work I do." But I say and think that nearly every day. These conversations have made me think about what contributes to high engagement at work and overall positive feelings about work and the company you work for. I've put my observations into a framework called the Three Cs. Those Cs are (1) Company and its values, (2) Core work, and (3) Colleagues. I believe when these Three Cs are high, employees will be proud to work for the organization and stay for a long time. Let me explain.

The Three Cs of Work Engagement

Company and its values
Colleagues
Core work

The first element to look for in a company is its mission and values. What is the purpose of the company? Is it just to make a profit, or does it go beyond that? Do they have a service mindset—to serve their clients and to serve their employees? Do they do more than just saying people are first—do they live it out, every day? I believe that when a company's values align with your values, you are in the right place. It is the starting place for the other Cs.

The second element to look for in a company is the core work—the work itself. What is primary job that you will be doing? Does it align with your talents and experience? Could you do that job every day, five days a week, and never get tired of it? Or is it something to do to get a paycheck, but you hate going to work—you can't wait until the day is over. Feeling that you are adding value in the work that you are doing is critical to high engagement.

Finally, the third element to look for in a company is the colleagues you are working with. It really comes down to this: do you love the people that you work with? Are you able to gracefully push and encourage them to achieve high performance? Do they find ways to push and encourage you to achieve high performance? Are you a better person and growing because you are part of a team of great colleagues? To be fully engaged at work, I believe it is important to love the people you work with and those who work for you.

In my experience, I have found that when these Three Cs are high, you feel good, possibly great, about your job and the company you work for. Sometimes you go through seasons when maybe one of the Cs is not at the top. If it is just a season, it will be ok. But, over a long period of time, it can wear on you. If you are in a job where two or three of the Cs are not positive, it is typically not a place you will stay for very long. And you certainly won't be proud to tell your friends about where you work.

For me, the Three Cs have always been positive at TIER1. I love everything about the company. The story of leukemia and the story of TiER1 just seem to go together—it's woven into the fabric of TiER1. TiER1 wanted to be in the battle with me, and they were. I hope we are all better people for taking the journey together. I know I am.

CHAPTER TEN

Finding Meaning in the Amazed Journey

During my initial stay in Penrose Hospital in 2010, I decided to start journaling about my experience. I recognized I would have a lot of time to read, reflect, and pray during the 30 days I would be in the hospital. Here I share some of the most significant journal entries I wrote during that time and some years later. Most of these are written in present tense, as I was experiencing these moments in the hospital or during my recovery at home.

Amazed

The inspiration for the title of this book, the cover image, and my entire story, is this word, Amazed. About a week into my initial 30-day stay at Penrose Hospital, in the evening when all was quiet on my floor, I was reading in Mark 7. This is where Jesus healed a deaf and mute man, and many others.

> "People were overwhelmed with
> amazement. He has done everything
> well, they said. He even makes the deaf
> hear and the mute speak." (Mark 7:37)

It was these words in verse 37 that were particularly powerful to me: "People were overwhelmed with amazement." Since all was quiet on the floor, I got up from the bed and walked to the window where I had an incredible view of Pikes Peak. At that very moment, I was listening to the song *Amazed* by Jared Anderson. Jared Anderson is a Christian worship leader and sometimes leads worship at our church—New Life Church in Colorado Springs. The key words of the chorus go like this:

Lord I am amazed by You

Lord I am amazed by You

Lord I am amazed by You

How you love me[5]

At a later part in the song, these words are found, based on Ephesians 3:18:

How wide, how deep, how great is your

love for me

All of a sudden, I found myself in an incredible emotional experience listening to this song. I felt the deep love of God like I had never experienced it before. His love came in like ocean waves—each one so powerful it took my breath away. His love was so powerful and overwhelming, I remember uttering these words: "Lord, you have to turn that down—it is too much for me to take in."

I'm not even sure how long this moment lasted. It slowly slipped away and I found myself bending down to get on my knees, while still looking out the window at Pikes Peak, wondering what just happened. It made me think back a few years ago when Debbie and I visited our former pastor, Mark Fuller, who was a pastor in Grove City, Ohio. Debbie and I were back in Cincinnati for a company Christmas party and decided to go see him on a Sunday. One of the key points I remember Pastor Mark talking about was God's amazing love. He said, "When you really come to understand how much God loves you, it will totally transform your life." I have always known God loves me, but not until this first week in the hospital have I ever experienced the overwhelming deepness of His love that moved me to tears. The feeling was an overwhelming sense of God in the room with me. A very tangible feeling that He was there watching me experience His love.

Why would He send such an outpouring of His love and presence to me? I'm nobody. Just an average guy who wants to be a good worker, a good husband, a good father, and a follower of Christ. That night I was totally amazed by His love, and I still am.

---APPLICATION---

What amazes you about the love of Jesus? Think of a time when you were reading about one of the miracles that Jesus performed. Reflect on this thought: that same Jesus knows and sees you.

Trusting Your Faith

At the top of Chapter One of 1 Peter, I have these words written: "Faith that has not been tested, cannot be trusted." I don't even remember the context for when I wrote those words down. But it must have made enough of an impact on me to write them there in my Bible. The context for these words is associated with verses 6 and 7:

> "In all this you greatly rejoice, though
> now for a little while you may have had
> to suffer grief in all kinds of trials.
> These have come so that the proven
> genuineness of your faith—of greater
> worth than gold, which perishes even
> though refined by fire—may result in
> praise, glory and honor when Jesus
> Christ is revealed." (1 Peter 1:6-7)

Because of my own battle with leukemia, I have been thinking about the suffering that is in our world and how it relates to our faith. It can be so easy to be discouraged in our own suffering or by watching the suffering of others. It can often rock the core of your faith and what you believe in. But that is what these verses are saying to us—there is no greater way to prove the genuineness of our faith than to experience suffering and trials. Until then, can we really know and trust our faith?

So, what do we do? Do we pray for the testing of our faith? And by praying that, do we get ready for suffering and trials to come our way? Jesus told us to be prepared for trouble in this world and to not base our faith on whether things are good in our life.

> "I have told you these things, so that in
> me you may have peace. In this world

you will have trouble. But take heart! I
have overcome the world." (John
16:33)

Suffering and trials are going to be in our lives, but our faith is in knowing that He has overcome the world. We know that He reigns in all of what is going on around us. The amazing thing is that Christ does not call us to this standard of faith and suffering without setting an example for us.

"To this you were called, because
Christ suffered for you, leaving you an
example, that you should follow in his
steps." (1 Peter 2:21)

We don't have to pray for suffering and trials to come our way. They are going to be there because it is part of the world we live in. But the best way to know if our faith can be trusted is to press through these times of testing and actually see that God has not left us alone. Saint Augustine said one of the most profound things on faith: "Faith is to believe what you do not see; the reward of this faith is to see what you believe."[6]

---APPLICATION---

Watch what happens the next time you are tested
and look for the reward of your faith. Then you
will know that your faith can be trusted. Offer a
prayer that asks God to prove your faith genuine
so that others can see that your faith is real and
not just something you mention with no meaning
behind it.

Be Quiet and Listen

The CEO (Greg Harmeyer) of the company I work for (TiER1 Performance Solutions) gave me a book by Mother Teresa titled *No Greater Love*. I've always admired the ministry of Mother Teresa but really never read much about her. She writes about prayer in one of the chapters. I've been thinking a lot about prayer, and especially how to really hear the voice of God in my life.

Mother Teresa captured what I have been thinking about in terms of listening. She says, "Listen in silence, because if your heart is full of other things you cannot hear the voice of God."[7] She goes on to say, "In the silence of the heart, God speaks and you have to listen. Then in the fullness of your heart, because it is full of God, full of love, full of compassion, full of faith, your mouth will speak." Her bottom line is that there are times when we need to withdraw into deeper silence and aloneness with God.

Most of the time, this cannot be done in our normal environment. I think we have to get away to a place of solitude. In Colorado, that is not hard to do—the mountains and the scenery are just beautiful and quiet. I just have not pursued the opportunity very often. I need to do that more so that the "noise of the world" doesn't invade the silence I am seeking. In a way, God has created that kind of environment for me during my hospital stays. At Penrose Hospital, I had an awesome view of the mountains, my own room, and the evenings were pretty quiet. It really helped me listen to God more than I ever have before.

---APPLICATION---

How much of your life is filled with noise? No wonder it is hard to hear God speak.

Find a place where you can find silence and be alone with God. Make it a place that is memorable—on a hiking trail, by a stream, looking out at a vast landscape. And in that moment, offer a prayer to the Lord that His voice would be strong and that everything else would fade into the background.

Iron Sharpens Iron

During my initial stay in Penrose Hospital, my best friend often stopped by. Kevin Dailey was my classmate at the United States Air Force Academy, and we graduated together in 1987. We were also roommates for our last two years at the Academy. I've heard someone say that it takes a long time to become old friends. Kevin is that friend. We were best man in each other's weddings after graduating from the Air Force Academy. We stayed in contact through our various assignments in the Air Force and as our families grew. Kevin and his family have been through their own very difficult times of loss, and he was genuine in his compassion and concern for my battle with leukemia.

For as long as I have known Kevin, he always knows how to bring a smile to my face. He is funny and likes to find ways to lighten up a difficult moment. On one of his visits to Penrose Hospital, Kevin came into my room and said, "Hey buddy, I've got a treat here from the outside world. It's a chocolate shake. I've made sure everything is clean so that this would be safe for you." I just laughed, and we both enjoyed our chocolate shakes together. It was exactly what I needed to break up the hospital food routine of the last three weeks.

Kevin is someone I can rely on. He is faithful to his word and genuinely cares about all the friends in his life. He reminds me of these verses in Proverbs:

> "As iron sharpens iron, so one person
> sharpens another." (Proverbs 27:17)

> "One who has unreliable friends soon
> comes to ruin, but there is a friend who
> sticks closer than a brother." (Proverbs
> 18:24)

I am a better man because of the friendship with Kevin. God knew I needed him right now in my darkest hour. I know

God had a hand in getting him an Air Force assignment back here to Colorado Springs so he could support me through this journey.

---APPLICATION---

Think through your friendships and identify the ones who you can really rely on—the ones that stick closer than a brother or sister.

Have you told them lately how much they mean to you?

Have you given to the friendship as much as they have given to you?

No Pain, No Gain

About three weeks into my initial stay at Penrose Hospital, I was experiencing some pain in my hip and buttocks (ok, that is where it was), I was asking the Lord, *What is this about?* I didn't understand why, after weeks of staying "boring" for the doctors, I would now have some unexplained pain. It was just an annoying pain that made it hard to sleep. The nurse gave me some pain medication and I quickly went to sleep.

I woke up one morning and I could still feel it, although at a pretty minor level. I just didn't know what was causing this as nothing in my status had really changed. When I mentioned it to the doctor and showed where the pain was primarily located, he said, "That could be an indication of something starting to develop in your bone marrow."

That gave me an interesting thought: *Could this pain be a sign of new life in my bone marrow?* Only time would tell. But I remembered back to an old saying, "No pain, No gain." Probably everyone has heard of that. And then I was thinking of my own journey the last few weeks. How God is able to take our pain, challenges, and disappointments, and turn them into something He can use for His glory. Something where at the end we have been refined. Maybe that is what is going on here. It reminds me of these words:

> "Dear friends, do not be surprised at
> the painful trial you are suffering, as
> though something strange were
> happening to you. But rejoice that you
> participate in the sufferings of Christ,
> so that you may be overjoyed when his
> glory is revealed." (1 Peter 4:12-13)

The gain is Christ's gain and we get to be participants in what He is doing in and through us.

---APPLICATION---

What is your disappointment right now that seems to bring pain into your life? Ask God to take that pain and transform it into something that can be used for His glory.

The Name of Jesus

Debbie and all of our children were with me one morning, visiting me at Penrose Hospital. Zachary (3 years old at this time) has a short attention span so we often had a Veggie Tales or a Leap Frog video for him to watch while he is at the hospital. Someone in our family would often take him for a walk to see the fish tank down the hall.

Debbie took him for a walk down the hallway of the hospital one morning and they went to the end of the hall near my room where there is a small prayer room. Debbie told Zachary that this was a prayer room and they needed to be quiet. Zachary entered the room with Debbie and folded his hands and bowed his head. Then he looked up at Debbie and said, "Mommy, I forgot my words." Debbie reminded him of the words and Zachary continued to bow his head and said, "Dear Jesus, help Daddy feel better." Innocent, sweet words from a 3-year old. I thought about the name of Jesus and how many people have called on that name and the miracles that have resulted from just His name. I don't understand it all, but somehow I know there is power and peace in calling on the name of Jesus, just like our little Zachary did.

---APPLICATION---

Have you thought about the wonderful name of Jesus and all that He has done for you? We all needed to be rescued by a savior. Without Jesus, we would be lost forever. Thank Him now for what He has done for you and experience the comfort of calling out His name.

Producing Perseverance

Sometimes I wonder what trials are all about and even how much we can suffer through in this world. It sure is easier to go through life without these challenges. But then I am always encouraged by the testimony of others who have walked through trials and their faith encourages me. Testing does produce perseverance as we learn from James, Chapter 1:

> Consider it pure joy, my brothers and
> sisters, whenever you face trials of
> many kinds, because you know that the
> testing of your faith produces
> perseverance. (James 1:2-3)

Even our Lord Jesus Christ had to endure His own anguish before going to the cross.

> During the days of Jesus' life on earth,
> he offered up prayers and petitions with
> fervent cries and tears to the one who
> could save him from death, and he was
> heard because of his reverent
> submission. Son though he was, he
> learned obedience from what he
> suffered. (James 5:7-8)

Even Jesus, the Son of God, cried to His heavenly father. He knew His mission and knew that He could not be spared from the cross, even though He wanted to in His human body. Because He persevered, we are able to have a savior that brings us back to God. He is able to sympathize with our weaknesses as we see in Hebrews 4:15. I personalized this scripture so I could hear God talking right to me:

Terence, you do not have a high priest
who is unable to sympathize with **your**
weaknesses, but **Terence you** have one
who has been tempted in every way,
just as **you** are—yet was without sin."
(adapted from Hebrews 4:15)

---APPLICATION---

Are you about at the end of your rope with the
testing that you are going through in life?

Recognize that Jesus Christ also faced trials and
temptations and knows what you are going
through. He is with you and He is for you.

Offer a prayer that recognizes Jesus went through
His own suffering. Tell God that you are thankful
for that example and that it gives you hope to
accept your own trial and be guided through it by
the God of creation.

He Forgives and Heals Us

One of the scriptures that has really meant a lot to me in understanding healing is found in Psalm 103:

> "Praise the LORD, O my soul, and
> forget not all his benefits. Who forgives
> all your sins and heals all your
> diseases." (Psalm 103:2-3)

In this verse I see this aspect of both forgiveness and healing mentioned at the same time. Jesus went to the cross to both save us and heal us. God is not the author of our sickness. He is all about healing and restoration. That makes so much sense. I just think about how I have missed out on communicating this to others in need because I didn't really understand the depth of His love and how much He wants to rid us of sickness. He just wants us to ask. He stands ready to do this more often than we might think. It doesn't take overwhelming faith. This is shown in Matthew 17 where Jesus is talking to His disciples:

> "He replied, 'Because you have so little
> faith. I tell you the truth, if you have
> faith as small as a mustard seed, you
> can say to this mountain, move from
> here to there and it will move. Nothing
> will be impossible for you.'" (Matthew
> 17:20)

Just a little bit of faith is all it takes. I just need to believe what He said and move on in faith knowing that He has taken care of it.

---APPLICATION---

Claim Psalm 103 right now and recognize that God does forgive all your sins and heals all your diseases. Ask God to strengthen your faith.

Offer a prayer right now thanking God for sustaining you during every tough time in your life.

Just Ask

Luke 11 is a very familiar scripture to many of us who grew up in the church:

> Ask and it will be given to you; seek
> and you will find; knock and the door
> will be opened to you. For everyone
> that asks receives; he who seeks finds;
> and to him who knocks, the door will
> be opened. (Luke 11:9-10)

I have known this verse since I was an early Christian. It is a classic and something often found in many sermons. I'm not sure how often I have really known the heart of God to ask of something big spiritually. I've asked for many things in the normal day-to-day activities: "Lord, help me to get through this traffic." "Help me in this job interview." "Please help rescue my mistake."

Those kinds of questions and the answers to them really don't take me closer to God. They are such small things. I'm sure God cares about all the day-to-day stuff I go through. But, I'm learning that He really cares about the relationship I have with Him. He wants me to draw closer to Him and the way to do that is to ask, seek, and knock about both the big and small things of life.

I really think He wants me to go after the big questions— the things that seem impossible, especially in healing and my relationship with Him. And I think He really wants me to learn to listen for His voice. That is tough. How do I know it is really Him who is answering these questions? I have to practice asking and I have to practice at listening. That is the only way to know the heart of God.

---APPLICATION---

Think back to a time when you really felt God whisper something to you. What were the characteristics of that experience? You probably were at a point in your relationship where you felt very close to God. You were studying His word. You were in an attitude of prayer and worship. You heard this whisper, or were impressed with a very clear thought, because you were connected in relationship.

Right now, enter into a time of prayer and worship. Linger in this time. Ask God to speak to your heart. Practice asking and practice listening.

TERENCE ANDRE

God's Word Will Help You in Your Time of Need

I could always tell when my blood counts were low, and I
remember one particular morning in the hospital when this
happened. I got really weak and I didn't feel like getting up. It's
how you feel if you have ever been on a long fast—the energy
is all gone. I received a blood transfusion and it gave me a
boost for a couple of days. A blood transfusion is like getting a
high energy cool drink after being exhausted and dehydrated. I
could not do this in my own strength. I had to call on God's
strength every day to make it through this. He has done so
much for me. Not just in this challenge, but throughout my life
of knowing Him.

A friend of mine who lost a child once told me that
everything you have learned in Sunday school, church, and
personal study really comes to aid you in a time of crisis. In
other words, the disciplines and patterns you develop in your
walk of faith will be there when you need it most. I feel that
now.

I feel the training and study about God and my Christian
faith when I was young and through my adult life came
together to help me during my battle with leukemia. It is the
rock I am standing on. Everything else seemed to waste away,
but the scriptures I memorized throughout my life and my
experience of walking with God is holding me up. He never
has left me in all these years and I've never felt closer to Him
than I am right now.

"I have hidden your word in my heart
that I might not sin against you."
(Psalm 119:11)

---APPLICATION---

Do you have verses from the Bible memorized that bring life to your soul and give you wisdom in living every day?

If you don't, start writing down your favorite Bible verses on small cards, memorize them, and keep them close so they are embedded in everything you do.

Becoming Like Little Children

> "And he said: 'I tell you the truth,
> unless you change and become like little
> children, you will never enter the
> kingdom of heaven. Therefore,
> whoever humbles himself like this child
> is the greatest in the kingdom of
> heaven.'" (Matthew 18:3-4)

Debbie and I were talking about this verse one night and I asked myself, I wonder what Jesus saw in little children that relates so closely to the kingdom of heaven? What are the characteristics of little children that we should model? After thinking about it for a few minutes, I started listing off characteristics of little children that I admire. Here they are:

1. They wake up every morning with a smile and forget about all the burdens of yesterday.

2. They come back for more love, even when they have been disciplined.

3. They run into your lap when you have been gone for any length of time.

4. They will sit on your lap and let you read for hours to them.

5. They see enjoyment in the simplest of things.

6. They go to bed with peace.

7. They wake up with peace.

8. They receive gifts with the most amazing smile and gratitude.

9. They go on, even when the world is not fair to them.

10. They trust without questioning.

These are just a few of the characteristics I thought of; I'm sure there are many more. There are so many lessons we can learn from little children in relation to our Heavenly Father. Is this what Jesus saw in little children when He asked us to become like them? He thought it so important that He said we would not see the kingdom of heaven unless we became like little children. Don't we let the world so consume us that there is no "childlike" left in us anymore? We are letting this world steal it away. I think we would fully experience God's love for us if we really focused on these childlike characteristics. We would wake up every morning with a smile and we would enjoy every day in the quietness of just being with Jesus.

---APPLICATION---

What is your favorite memory as a child? Imagine Jesus watching you in that memorable event, and the smile He would have on His face. That's how He sees you now.

Stay With It

Something incredible happened about two years after transplant, and right away it made me think of God's faithfulness. One morning I woke up and was playing with my wedding band. It surprised me that it came off so easily. Since transplant I have had some form of swelling in my arms, legs, and fingers. I even had my ring sized up two different times. It is just a form of the graft vs. host disease (GVHD) that is often common from bone marrow transplant. My doctor always told me that it would eventually burn its way out. It could take months or years. "Just stick with it," he would say. In my case it has been over two years. But when I saw my ring slip off so easily, I also noticed that all of my other swelling was literally gone. I could bend my legs to a fuller range, my fingers were not puffy, and my watch fit like it used to. Just like that, the effects of GVHD were gone. It was a long wait. I couldn't will it to happen. I had to be patient. But I did trust my doctor's word that it would eventually go away and I focused on that.

I wondered if the bible had anything to say about "staying with it" and the transformation we can count on if we are disciplined followers of Jesus Christ. James 1:12 was the first verse that came up in my searching.

> "Happy are those who remain faithful
> under trials, because when they succeed
> in passing such a test, they will receive
> as their reward the life which God has
> promised to those who love him."
> (James 1:12, Good News Version)

It is important to remain faithful, even when we may not be seeing the dramatic results we want, and the timing that we want. Two years was a long time. But there was nothing I could do to accelerate the process. I just had to stay with it. I was confident that the change, the transformation, would eventually happen. Philippians reminds us of that.

> "Being confident of this, that he who
> began a good work in you will carry it
> on to completion until the day of Christ
> Jesus." (Philippians 1:6)

Jesus wants to complete through us and in us what He started. So, don't be discouraged if you have endured something for years. Keep your focus on what Jesus has said He will do. And stay with it.

---APPLICATION---

What are you about ready to give up on—a promise that you have carried with you for a long time? Put that promise in the hands of Jesus and let Him complete what He said He would do.

This Will Be So Easy For Me To Do

This is a part of my story that only a few people know about. I held onto it for many years, especially after the brain tumor, as I wasn't sure of the reality of this experience. About two weeks into that first hospital stay, I remember walking down to the end of the hallway where there was a window. Looking out, I started a conversation with God about the heaviness I felt over the disease I was fighting. I had lots of questions. How would my family deal with this? Would this be the end? Would I see my children get married and have grandchildren? Would I ever walk out of this hospital? I sought answers from the God who saved me as a young boy. I paused for a long time, waiting for an impression from God, for an answer. It wasn't long before I heard these words: "This will be so easy for me to do." Those words were not audible, but I could feel, deep in my soul, that God had delivered that answer to my very direct question— was I going to live through this? I'm not sure how much time went by before I decided to see if I could confirm God's promise. I think it was just a few seconds, and I don't even know where this thought came from, but I wanted some assurance that God delivered those words to me, and not something I thought up. So, I answered back: "If this is going to be so easy for you to do, then let me walk out of this hospital with my hair—don't let me lose my hair."

As most of us probably know or have seen, many people lose their hair from chemo treatment. Chemo is known to kill all rapidly dividing cells. Our hair follicles are highly active cells that frequently divide to produce growing hair. So, hair often becomes the unfortunate bystander that takes the fall along with the cancer cells. Hair loss, for many, is one of the most traumatic experiences of cancer. But, let's be honest, it is likely more traumatic for women. It's not that big of a deal to see a bald man. In fact, many men look great bald. And some men, for style, shave all their remaining hair off instead of having patches of hair growing in some spots and none elsewhere. With that in mind, I don't know why holding onto my hair was the request I made, other than it being a very visible thing I could count on, and that others could see.

So, that's the request I made. I really didn't think much about it until I left the hospital. But I left the hospital with my hair! It was still closely cut and did thin out a bit, but it was still there. We had a friend give me a "buzz" cut when I first arrived in the hospital thinking that I would lose it anyway and it would be better to lose a thin layer of hair than big chunks. I then thought: *Wow, God must have really said those words because I walked out of the hospital with my hair.*

That thought stayed with me until my relapse in 2011. During my relapse, I often went back to God and reminded Him of what He told me in February 2010, "This will be so easy for me to do." I wondered what the relapse was all about? Then, four years went by from 2011-2015 where I was completely free from leukemia. Life was good. God's promise was true. But, I then experienced a brain tumor in 2015 and leukemia was found in that tumor. I remember thinking, "God, you said this would be so easy for you to do. Explain the relapse and now the brain tumor. This doesn't feel that easy. In fact, it's been pretty hard."

I've carried this question with me for the last few years, especially since the brain tumor in 2015. I was certain I heard those words, that promise in 2010. I just knew it in my heart. But none of this has been easy. Not on me and not for our family. Only recently have I been given a different perspective on this. One morning I was reading in Luke 22, after Jesus and His disciples have the Last Supper, and Jesus knows that He will soon go to the cross and die. My attention was drawn to verses 41-44:

> "He withdrew about a stone's throw
> beyond them, knelt down and prayed,
> 'Father, if you are willing, take this cup
> from me; yet not my will, but yours be
> done.' An angel from heaven appeared

to him and strengthened him. And
being in anguish, he prayed more
earnestly, and his sweat was like drops
of blood falling to the ground." (Luke
22:41-44)

Jesus was in anguish as He faced the reality of the cross. And then I felt this revelation in that moment: It was easy for God to raise His son Jesus to life again, but the journey was not easy on Jesus. It was as if God was saying to me, "Terence, I said this would be so EASY FOR ME TO DO. I know it has been tough on you, but I have been with you—I've never forsaken you (see Deuteronomy 31:6). Here you are alive and enjoying life to the fullest. You have a great job, working for a great company. You have walked your daughter down the aisle at her wedding, seen your oldest son graduate from the Air Force Academy and also get married. You have two beautiful grandchildren and one more on the way. You celebrated your 30th wedding anniversary last year with your high school sweetheart. My promises are true."

I still don't know why I have had to go through a relapse and a brain tumor. But I can cling to this: God has been with me. As a young boy, He saved me from spiritual death and now almost certain physical death from leukemia. He has prolonged my life when there was no hope for the future. What have you heard God promise to you? Know He is with you and will see it to completion until the day of Christ Jesus (see Philippians 1:6).

---APPLICATION---

What promise are you holding onto from God?
Something that you are sure you heard from God,
but have not seen the evidence of that promise?
Take a moment to go to God with that promise
and take confidence in this verse:

"Whatever God has promised gets stamped with the Yes of Jesus. In him, this is what we preach and pray, the great Amen, God's Yes and our Yes together, gloriously evident. God affirms us, making us a sure thing in Christ, putting his Yes within us. By his Spirit he has stamped us with his eternal pledge—a sure beginning of what he is destined to complete." (2 Corinthians 1:20-22, MSG)

It's the Hard that Makes it Great

This experience with leukemia, bone marrow transplant, and a brain tumor was a tough journey that shaped our entire family. A pastor once told me, "At the beginning of the test, faith is challenged. At the end of the test, faith is rewarded. But in the middle of the test faith is strengthened." I love the way The Message version puts it:

> "Consider it a sheer gift, friends, when
> tests and challenges come at you from
> all sides. You know that under pressure,
> your faith-life is forced into the open
> and shows its true colors. So don't try
> to get out of anything prematurely. Let
> it do its work so you become mature
> and well-developed, not deficient in any
> way. If you don't know what you're
> doing, pray to the Father. He loves to
> help. You'll get his help, and won't be
> condescended to when you ask for it.
> Ask boldly, believingly, without a
> second thought" (James 1:2-5, MSG)

What is it about going through challenges and coming out on the other side more mature and refined? Remember the 1992 movie *A League of Their Own* starring Geena Davis and Tom Hanks? There's a scene where Dottie (Geena Davis) tells Jimmy (Tom Hanks) that she is going home to Oregon instead of playing with the team in the league's world series. Jimmy tries to persuade her to stay, but Dottie responds, "It just got too hard." Jimmy's next line has stayed with me over the years:

"The hard is what makes it great."[8]

There is something to be said about embracing and

overcoming a challenge. Whatever your personal feelings on Alabama Crimson Tide or their coach, Nick Saban, I think he got it exactly right when he said this after winning the 2018 National Championship against Georgia:

"If you can't overcome hard, you're
never going to have any great victories
in your life."[9]

It is a true miracle that I survived. I know our days are numbered, but I really wanted to walk my daughter, Jennifer down the aisle when she got married. I also wanted to see Brian graduate from the Air Force Academy. I wanted to watch Zachary grow up, go camping with him, take him through Boy Scouts, and do the things that fathers and sons do together.

The miracle is that I did get to walk Jennifer down the aisle in 2012; about a year after bone marrow transplant. I remember the smile I had on my face walking Jennifer down the aisle and recognizing what a glorious day it was to be alive. I also got to watch Brian graduate from the Air Force Academy and shake the hand of the Vice President of the United States. I am getting to enjoy life now with Zachary as he grows up. I am blessed.

---APPLICATION---

What in your life is hard right now? Are you
tempted to run away from it, to escape? Even
though that would be the easy way out, choose
the option of running into the challenge. You will
learn a lot more about yourself and you will be
grateful for embracing the challenge and
persevering.

Lessons Learned from Leukemia

Here are the lessons I have learned through my journey with leukemia:

First, God really loves us. We can know this even when life is at its worst. Reading through the New Testament while in the hospital for the initial 30 days, I took note of how many times the word "amazed" is mentioned. I counted 40. I certainly experienced the amazing love of God in a quiet hospital room on many occasions. One night in particular (on Day 5), I remember feeling God's amazing love flow over me like a crashing wave.

Second, God will be glorified, even in our sickness. He uses our story to speak into others and show the power of His love. Remember the story of the blind man who was healed? The disciples wondered who had sinned; the blind man or his parents. Look at Jesus' answer: "Neither this man nor his parents sinned," said Jesus, "but this happened so that the works of God might be displayed in him" (John 9:3). Both Debbie and I can testify to the fact of being able to glorify God through this story of leukemia, bone marrow transplant, and brain tumor by telling people that God was with us and He grew our faith.

Third, Press into God when life is at its worst. God does provide a way to endure when life comes after you. The last part of 1 Corinthians 10:13 says, "...but when you are tempted, he will also provide a way out so that you can stand up under it." So, lean into God, He will show you the way. My wife Debbie was the best example of this as I was going through my journey with leukemia. She also was suffering, as she watched her sick husband, wondered what the next day might hold, and trying to hold everything together at home. She went to her knees daily and Jesus met her there, helping her to make it through this journey.

AFTERWORD

by Jared Anderson

You've read this incredible story of how Terence found comfort, purpose, and light in a time of struggle most of us can't imagine. I want to tell you a little of what's behind the song *Amazed* that Terence referenced in this book.

I was just out of college and living back at home with my parents. This new-to-them house was comfortable and easy, but I was mystified as to how I was back here at square one and what was coming next for me. I loved music. Every night I would be at the piano outside my upstairs room in the loft playing, noodling, sound-tracking my imagination. I worked construction with my Dad one day a week and was helping out at our church in the music office, both of which felt lacking in the adventure and newness I was sure I was made for. I felt much more deeply than I was seeing in my opportunities, and I just couldn't figure out where to begin.

The three chords came to me one night that sounded like the style of longing that I desperately loved. And that one line "you dance over me while I am unaware" was where this was going. In the notes I found the truth my heart needed that my Heavenly Father was excited. He was moving not to the predictable tempo of 9 to 5 and paycheck to paycheck. He was moving in a dance, the response of muscles to emotion. Emotion in motion. He wanted to lead me on a path and not stick me in a position.

Over the next two weeks or so the song began to complete as I revisited and tried to describe the feel in lyrics. "You sing all around but I never hear the sound. Lord, I'm amazed by you how you love me."

Tension is necessary for life. Music moves from consonance to dissonance, from departure to resolution much like weather patterns. Harmony indicates difference. The uniqueness of my heart and desire against the landscape of my surrounding was the song *Amazed*. What I felt was a disappointing destination was an important and monumental location from which to sing and make melody. Announcing to my own soul that I'm worth dancing over. And though flummoxed in my mind as to how to flourish, I could be amazed in my heart at how His love hadn't given up.

His love longs to widen, deepen, open doors, and reveal more than any amount of money, any physical ecstasy, any human pleasure or security. His love is revealed through the tension not around it.

I would never have predicted what this cry-for-help song would end up becoming. I've sung it somewhere almost every week for 15 years. I'm still not sick of it. It's still true.

After reading this book you're probably Amazed at how Terence can be so positive and gracious after enduring these diseases. I am. And let me say that he's just as earnest and hopeful in person as he is in the story.

NOTES

1. Elliot, Elisabeth. *There's no coming to life without pain.* Accessed September 7, 2018, https://www.ligonier.org/learn/articles/theres-no-coming-life-without-pain-interview-elisabeth-elliot/.

2. Neander, Joachim. *Praise to the Lord, the Almighty.* Public domain, 1680.

3. Stevenson, Mary. *Footprints in the Sand.* 1936.

4. Inc. Magazine. *Best workplaces,* accessed September 4, 2018, https://www.inc.com/best-workplaces/list.

5. Anderson, Jared. *Amazed.* Brentwood, TN: Capitol CMG Publishing. Copyright © 2003 Integrity Worship Music (ASCAP) (adm. at CapitolCMGPublishing.com) All rights reserved. Used by permission.

6. St. Augustine of Hippo. *Sermones 4.1.1,* accessed August 30, 2018, https://en.wikiquote.org/wiki/Augustine_of_Hippo.

7. Teresa, Mother. *No Greater Love.* Novato, CA: New World Library, 2002.

8. *A League of Their Own.* DVD. Culver City, CA: Columbia Pictures Corporation, 1992.

9. ABC News. *Title win puts exclamation point on Bama's decade of dominance,* accessed January 15, 2018, https://abcnews.go.com/Sports/title-win-puts-exclamation-point-bamas-decade-dominance/story?id=52229054.

My family with me in the hospital during the first battle
with leukemia (Brian, Debbie, Zachary, me, Jennifer)

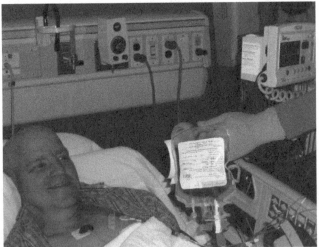

Looking at my sister's stem cells just a few minutes before
bone marrow transplant.

Walking Jennifer down the aisle a year after bone marrow transplant.

Commissioning Brian as a 2Lt in the Air Force.

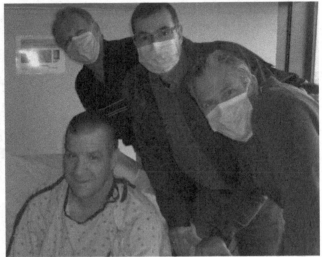

Three of the guys from my weekly devotional group for "man church" in the hospital (Todd Anderson, Dusty Rhodes, and Kurt Leander. Kevin Smith missing).

Dr. Gutman, my Bone Marrow Transplant doctor.

Dr. Youssef, my Neurosurgeon.

Dr. Pollyea, my leukemia doctor at Anschutz.

Dr. Murphy, my leukemia doctor at Penrose Hospital.

Carolyn Coleman, my primary nurse at Penrose Hospital.

A recent picture of our family, with Jennifer's husband (Andrew), Brian's wife (Kaitlyn), Zachary, and our three grandchildren (Eleanor, William, and Caleb).

ABOUT THE AUTHOR

Dr. Terence Andre is the Chief Scientist at TiER1 Performance Solutions. He joined TiER1 in 2008 after a full career in the Air Force as an engineer/scientist. Dr. Andre was an associate professor at the U.S. Air Force Academy where he taught courses in psychology and systems engineering. He retired as a Lieutenant Colonel after having served in systems acquisition, test and evaluation, research and development, and academics. Terence holds a Ph.D. in Industrial and Systems Engineering from Virginia Tech, a master's degree in Adult Education from Regis University, a master's degree in Industrial Engineering from California Polytechnic State University, and a bachelor's degree in Behavioral Sciences from the U.S. Air Force Academy.

Terence lives in Colorado Springs with his wife and youngest son. His daughter is married to an Air Force pilot and has three children. His oldest son is also married and serves as a pilot in the Air Force. Terence loves to snow ski, camp, mountain bike, and do just about anything outdoors in Colorado.

For additional thoughts about God's amazing love, you can read more at this site: www.amazedbyhislove.com.

AMAZED BY HIS LOVE

Made in USA - Kendallville, IN
1220620_9781728923895
01.04.2021 0818